Urbain Grandier

Alexandre Dumas

DODO PRESS

Urbain Grandier

Chapter I

On Sunday, the 26th of November, 1631, there was great excitement in the little town of Loudun, especially in the narrow streets which led to the church of Saint-Pierre in the marketplace, from the gate of which the town was entered by anyone coming from the direction of the abbey of Saint-Jouin-les-Marmes. This excitement was caused by the expected arrival of a personage who had been much in people's mouths latterly in Loudun, and about whom there was such difference of opinion that discussion on the subject between those who were on his side and those who were against him was carried on with true provincial acrimony. It was easy to see, by the varied expressions on the faces of those who turned the doorsteps into improvised debating clubs, how varied were the feelings with which the man would be welcomed who had himself formally announced to friends and enemies alike the exact date of his return.

About nine o'clock a kind of sympathetic vibration ran through the crowd, and with the rapidity of a flash of lightning the words, "There he is! there he is!" passed from group to group. At this cry some withdrew into their houses and shut their doors and darkened their windows, as if it were a day of public mourning, while others opened them wide, as if to let joy enter. In a few moments the uproar and confusion evoked by the news was succeeded by the deep silence of breathless curiosity.

Then, through the silence, a figure advanced, carrying a branch of laurel in one hand as a token of triumph. It was that of a young man of from thirty-two to thirty-four years of age, with a graceful and well-knit frame, an aristocratic air and faultlessly beautiful features of a somewhat haughty expression. Although he had walked three leagues to reach the town, the ecclesiastical garb which he wore was not only elegant but of dainty freshness. His eyes turned to heaven, and singing in a sweet voice praise to the Lord, he passed through the streets leading to the church in the market-place with a slow and solemn gait, without vouchsafing a look, a word, or a gesture to anyone. The entire crowd, falling into step, marched behind him as he advanced, singing like him, the singers being the prettiest girls in Loudun, for we have forgotten to say that the crowd consisted almost entirely of women.

Meanwhile the object of all this commotion arrived at length at the porch of the church of Saint-Pierre. Ascending the steps, he knelt at the top and prayed in a low voice, then rising he touched the church doors with his laurel branch, and they opened wide as if by magic, revealing the choir decorated and illuminated as if for one of the four great feasts of the year, and with all its scholars, choir boys, singers, beadles, and vergers in their places. Glancing around, he for whom they were waiting came up the nave, passed through the choir, knelt for a second time at the foot of the altar, upon which he laid the branch of laurel, then putting on a robe as white as snow and passing the stole around his neck, he began the celebration of the mass before a congregation composed of all those who had followed him. At the end of the mass a Te Deum was sung.

He who had just rendered thanks to God for his own victory with all the solemn ceremonial usually reserved for the triumphs of kings was the priest Urbain Grandier. Two days before, he had been acquitted, in virtue of a decision pronounced by M. d'Escoubleau de Sourdis, Archbishop of Bordeaux, of an accusation brought against him of which he had been declared guilty by a magistrate, and in punishment of which he had been condemned to fast on bread and water every Friday for three months, and forbidden to exercise his priestly functions in the diocese of Poitiers for five years and in the town of Loudun for ever.

These are the circumstances under which the sentence had been passed and the judgment reversed.

Urbain Grandier was born at Rovere, a village near Sable, a little town of Bas-Maine. Having studied the sciences with his father Pierre and his uncle Claude Grandier, who were learned astrologers and alchemists, he entered, at the age of twelve, the Jesuit college at Bordeaux, having already received the ordinary education of a young man. The professors soon found that besides his considerable attainments he had great natural gifts for languages and oratory; they therefore made of him a thorough classical scholar, and in order to develop his oratorical talent encouraged him to practise preaching. They soon grew very fond of a pupil who was likely to bring them so much credit, and as soon as he was old enough to take holy orders they gave him the cure of souls in the parish of Saint-Pierre in Loudun, which was in the gift of the college. When he had been some months installed there as a priest-in-charge, he received a prebendal stall, thanks to the same patrons, in the collegiate church of Sainte-Croix.

It is easy to understand that the bestowal of these two positions on so young a man, who did not even belong to the province, made him seem in some sort a usurper of rights and privileges belonging to the people of the country, and drew upon him the envy of his brother-ecclesiastics. There were, in fact, many other reasons why Urbain should be an object of jealousy to these: first, as we have already said, he was very handsome, then the instruction which he had received from his father had opened the world of science to him and given him the key to a thousand things which were mysteries to the ignorant, but which he fathomed with the greatest ease. Furthermore, the comprehensive course of study which he had followed at the Jesuit college had raised him above a crowd of prejudices, which are sacred to the vulgar, but for which he made no secret of his contempt; and lastly, the eloquence of his sermons had drawn to his church the greater part of the regular congregations of the other religious communities, especially of the mendicant orders, who had till then, in what concerned preaching, borne away the palm at Loudun. As we have said, all this was more than enough to excite, first jealousy, and then hatred. And both were excited in no ordinary degree.

We all know how easily the ill-natured gossip of a small town can rouse the angry contempt of the masses for everything which is beyond or above them. In a wider sphere Urbain would have shone by his many gifts, but, cooped up as he was within the walls of a little town and deprived of air and space, all that might have conduced to his success in Paris led to his destruction at Loudun.

Urbain Grandier

It was also unfortunate for Urbain that his character, far from winning pardon for his genius, augmented the hatred which the latter inspired. Urbain, who in his intercourse with his friends was cordial and agreeable, was sarcastic, cold, and haughty to his enemies. When he had once resolved on a course, he pursued it unflinchingly; he jealously exacted all the honour due to the rank at which he had arrived, defending it as though it were a conquest; he also insisted on enforcing all his legal rights, and he resented the opposition and angry words of casual opponents with a harshness which made them his lifelong enemies.

The first example which Urbain gave of this inflexibility was in 1620, when he gained a lawsuit against a priest named Meunier. He caused the sentence to be carried out with such rigour that he awoke an inextinguishable hatred in Meunier's mind, which ever after burst forth on the slightest provocation.

A second lawsuit, which he likewise gained; was one which he undertook against the chapter of Sainte-Croix with regard to a house, his claim to which the chapter, disputed. Here again he displayed the same determination to exact his strict legal rights to the last iota, and unfortunately Mignon, the attorney of the unsuccessful chapter, was a revengeful, vindictive, and ambitious man; too commonplace ever to arrive at a high position, and yet too much above his surroundings to be content with the secondary position which he occupied. This man, who was a canon of the collegiate church of Sainte-Croix and director of the Ursuline convent, will have an important part to play in the following narrative. Being as hypocritical as Urbain was straightforward, his ambition was to gain wherever his name was known a reputation for exalted piety; he therefore affected in his life the asceticism of an anchorite and the self-denial of a saint. As he had much experience in ecclesiastical lawsuits, he looked on the chapter's loss of this one, of which he had in some sort guaranteed the success, as a personal humiliation, so that when Urbain gave himself airs of triumph and exacted the last letter of his bond, as in the case of Meunier, he turned Mignon into an enemy who was not only more relentless but more dangerous than the former.

In the meantime, and in consequence of this lawsuit, a certain Barot, an uncle of Mignon and his partner as well, got up a dispute with Urbain, but as he was a man below mediocrity, Urbain required in order to crush him only to let fall from the height of his superiority a few of those disdainful words which brand as deeply as a red-hot iron. This man, though totally wanting in parts, was very rich, and having no children was always surrounded by a horde of relatives, every one of whom was absorbed in the attempt to make himself so agreeable that his name would appear in Barot's will. This being so, the mocking words which were rained down on Barot spattered not only himself but also all those who had sided with him in the quarrel, and thus added considerably to the tale of Urbain's enemies.

About this epoch a still graver event took place. Amongst the most assiduous frequenters of the confessional in his church was a young and pretty girl, Julie by name, the daughter of the king's attorney, Trinquant—Trinquant being, as well as Barot, an uncle of Mignon. Now it happened that this young girl fell into such a state of debility that she was obliged to keep her room. One of her friends, named Marthe Pelletier, giving up society, of which she was very fond, undertook to nurse the patient, and carried her devotion so far as to shut herself up in the same room with her. When Julie Trinquant had recovered and was able again to take her place in the world, it came out that Marthe Pelletier, during her weeks of retirement, had given birth to a child, which had been baptized and then put out to nurse. Now, by one of those odd whims which so often take possession of the public mind, everyone in Loudun persisted in asserting that the real mother of the infant was not she who had acknowledged herself as such—that, in short, Marthe Pelletier had sold her good name to her friend Julie for a sum of money; and of course it followed as a matter about which there could be no possible doubt, that Urbain was the father.

Trinquant hearing of the reports about his daughter, took upon himself as king's attorney to have Marthe Pelletier arrested and imprisoned. Being questioned about the child, she insisted that she was its mother, and would take its maintenance upon herself. To have brought a child into the world under such circumstances was a sin, but not a crime; Trinquant was therefore obliged to set Marthe at liberty, and the abuse of justice of which he was guilty served only to spread the scandal farther and to strengthen the public in the belief it had taken up.

Hitherto, whether through the intervention of the heavenly powers, or by means of his own cleverness, Urbain Grandier had come out victor in every struggle in which he had engaged, but each victor had added to the number of his enemies, and these were now so numerous that any other than he would have been alarmed, and have tried either to conciliate them or to take precautions against their malice; but Urbain, wrapped in his pride, and perhaps conscious of his innocence, paid no attention to the counsels of his most faithful followers, but went on his way unheeding.

All the opponents whom till now Urbain had encountered had been entirely unconnected with each other, and had each struggled for his own individual ends. Urbain's enemies, believing that the cause of his success was to be found in the want of cooperation among themselves, now determined to unite in order to crush him. In consequence, a conference was held at Barot's, at which, besides Barot himself, Meunier, Trinquant, and Mignon took part, and the latter had also brought with him one Menuau, a king's counsel and his own most intimate friend, who was, however, influenced by other motives than friendship in joining the conspiracy. The fact was, that Menuau was in love with a woman who had steadfastly refused to show him any favour, and he had got firmly fixed in his head that the reason for her else inexplicable indifference and disdain was that Urbain had been beforehand with him in finding an entrance to her heart. The object of the meeting was to agree as to the best means of driving the common enemy out of Loudon and its neighbourhood.

Urbain's life was so well ordered that it presented little which his enemies could use as a handle for their purpose. His only foible seemed to be a predilection for female society; while in return all the wives and daughters of the place, with the unerring instinct of their sex, seeing, that the new priest was young, handsome, and eloquent, chose him, whenever it was possible, as their spiritual director. As this preference had already offended many husbands and fathers, the decision the conspirators arrived at was that on this side alone was Grandier vulnerable, and that their only chance of success was to attack him where he was weakest. Almost at once, therefore, the vague reports which had been floating about began to attain a certain definiteness: there were allusions made, though no name was mentioned, to a young girl in Loudun; who in spite of Grandier's frequent unfaithfulness yet remained his mistress-in- chief; then it began to be whispered that the young girl, having had conscientious scruples about her love for Urbain, he had allayed them by an act of sacrilege—that is to say, he had, as priest, in the middle of the night, performed the service of marriage between himself and his mistress. The more absurd the reports, the more credence did they gain, and it was not long till everyone in Loudun believed them true, although no one was able to name the mysterious heroine of the tale who had had the courage to contract a marriage with a priest; and considering how small Loudun was, this was most extraordinary.

Resolute and full of courage as was Grandier, at length he could not conceal from himself that his path lay over quicksands: he felt that slander was secretly closing him round, and that as soon as he was well entangled in her shiny folds, she would reveal herself by raising her abhorred head, and that then a mortal combat between them would begin. But it was one of his convictions that to draw back was to acknowledge one's guilt; besides, as far as he was concerned, it was probably too late for him to retrace his steps. He therefore went on his way, as unyielding, as scornful, and as haughty as ever.

Among those who were supposed to be most active in spreading the slanders relative to Urbain was a man called Duthibaut, a person of importance in the province, who was supposed by the townspeople to hold very advanced views, and who was a "Sir Oracle" to whom the commonplace and vulgar turned for enlightenment. Some of this man's strictures on Grandier were reported to the latter, especially some calumnies to which Duthibaut had given vent at the Marquis de Bellay's; and one day, Grandier, arrayed in priestly garments, was about to enter the church of Sainte-Croix to assist in the service, he encountered Duthibaut at the entrance, and with his usual haughty disdain accused him of slander. Duthibaut, who had got into the habit of saying and doing whatever came into his head without fear of being called to account, partly because of his wealth and partly because of the influence he had gained over the narrow-minded, who are so numerous in a small provincial town, and who regarded him as being much above them, was so furious at this public reprimand, that he raised his cane and struck Urbain.

The opportunity which this affront afforded Grandier of being revenged on all his enemies was too precious to be neglected, but, convinced, with too much reason, that he would never obtain justice from the local authorities, although the respect due to the Church had been infringed, in his person he decided to appeal to King Louis XIII, who deigned to receive him, and deciding that the insult offered to a priest robed in the sacred vestments should be expiated, sent the cause to the high court of Parliament, with instructions that the case against Duthibaut should be tried and decided there.

Hereupon Urbain's enemies saw they had no time to lose, and took advantage of his absence to make counter accusations against him. Two worthies beings, named Cherbonneau and Bugrau, agreed to become informers, and were brought before the ecclesiastical magistrate at Poitiers. They accused Grandier of having corrupted women and girls, of indulging in blasphemy and profanity, of neglecting to read his breviary daily, and of turning God's sanctuary into a place of debauchery and prostitution. The information was taken down, and Louis Chauvet, the civil lieutenant, and the archpriest of Saint- Marcel and the Loudenois, were appointed to investigate the matter, so that, while Urbain was instituting proceedings against Duthibaut in Paris, information was laid against himself in Loudun. This matter thus set going was pushed forward with all the acrimony so common in religious prosecutions; Trinquant appeared as a witness, and drew many others after him, and whatever omissions were found in the depositions were interpolated according to the needs of the prosecution. The result was that the case when fully got up appeared to be so serious that it was sent to the Bishop of Poitiers for trial. Now the bishop was not only surrounded by the friends of those who were bringing the accusations against Grandier, but had himself a grudge against him. It had happened some time before that Urbain, the case being urgent, had dispensed with the usual notice of a marriage, and the bishop, knowing this, found in the papers laid before him, superficial as they were, sufficient evidence against Urbain to justify him in issuing a warrant for his apprehension, which was drawn up in the following words:

"Henri-Louis, Chataignier de la Rochepezai, by divine mercy Bishop of Poitiers, in view of the charges and informations conveyed to us by the archpriest of Loudun against Urbain Grandier, priest-in-charge of the Church of Saint-Pierre in the Market-Place at Loudun, in virtue of a commission appointed by us directed to the said archpriest, or in his absence to the Prior of Chassaignes, in view also of the opinion given by our attorney upon the said charges, have ordered and do hereby order that Urbain Grandier, the accused, be quietly taken to the prison in our palace in Poitiers, if it so be that he be taken and apprehended, and if not, that he be summoned to appear at his domicile within three days, by the first apparitor-priest, or tonsured clerk, and also by the first royal sergeant, upon this warrant, and we request the aid of the secular authorities, and to them, or to any one of them, we hereby give power and authority to carry out this decree notwithstanding any opposition or appeal, and the said Grandier having been heard, such a decision will be given by our attorney as the facts may seem to warrant.

"Given at Dissay the 22nd day of October 1629, and signed in the original as follows:

"HENRI-LOUIS, Bishop of Poitiers."

Grandier was, as we have said, at Paris when these proceedings were taken against him, conducting before the Parliament his case against Duthibaut. The latter received a copy of the decision arrived at by the bishop, before Grandier knew of the charges that had been formulated against him, and having in the course of his defence drawn a terrible picture of the immorality of Grandier's life, he produced as a proof of the truth of his assertions the damning document which had been put into his hands. The court, not knowing what to think of the turn affairs had taken, decided that before considering the accusations brought by Grandier, he must appear before his bishop to clear himself of the charges, brought against himself. Consequently he left Paris at once, and arrived at Loudun, where he only stayed long enough to learn what had happened in his absence, and then went on to Poitiers in order to draw up his defence. He had, however, no sooner set foot in the place than he was arrested by a sheriff's officer named Chatry, and confined in the prison of the episcopal palace.

It was the middle of November, and the prison was at all times cold and damp, yet no attention was paid to Grandier's request that he should be transferred to some other place of confinement. Convinced by this that his enemies had more influence than he had supposed, he resolved to possess his soul in patience, and remained a prisoner for two months, during which even his warmest friends believed him lost, while Duthibaut openly laughed at the proceedings instituted against himself, which he now believed would never go any farther, and Barot had already selected one of his heirs, a certain Ismael Boulieau, as successor to Urbain as priest and prebendary.

It was arranged that the costs of the lawsuit should be defrayed out of a fund raised by the prosecutors, the rich paying for the poor; for as all the witnesses lived at Loudun and the trial was to take place at Poitiers, considerable expense would be incurred by the necessity of bringing so many people such a distance; but the lust of vengeance proved stronger than the lust of gold; the subscription expected from each being estimated according to his fortune, each paid without a murmur, and at the end of two months the case was concluded.

In spite of the evident pains taken by the prosecution to strain the evidence against the defendant, the principal charge could not be sustained, which was that he had led astray many wives and daughters in Loudun. No one woman came forward to complain of her ruin by Grandier; the name of no single victim of his alleged immorality was given. The conduct of the case was the most extraordinary ever seen; it was evident that the accusations were founded on hearsay and not on fact, and yet a decision and sentence against Grandier were pronounced on January 3rd, 1630. The sentence was as follows: For three months to fast each Friday on bread and water by way of penance; to be inhibited from the performance of clerical functions in the diocese of Poitiers for five years, and in the town of Loudun for ever.

Both parties appealed from this decision: Grandier to the Archbishop of Bordeaux, and his adversaries, on the advice of the attorney to the diocese, pleading a miscarriage of justice, to the Parliament of Paris; this last appeal being made in order to overwhelm Grandier and break his spirit. But Grandier's resolution enabled him to face this attack boldly: he engaged counsel to defend his case before the Parliament, while he himself conducted his appeal to the Archbishop of Bordeaux. But as there were many necessary witnesses, and it was almost impossible to bring them all such a great distance, the archiepiscopal court sent the appeal to the presidial court of Poitiers. The public prosecutor of Poitiers began a fresh investigation, which being conducted with impartiality was not encouraging to Grandier's accusers. There had been many conflicting statements made by the witnesses, and these were now repeated: other witnesses had declared quite openly that they had been bribed; others again stated that their depositions had been tampered with; and amongst these latter was a certain priest named Mechin, and also that Ishmael Boulieau whom Barot had been in such a hurry to select as candidate for the reversion of Grandier's preferments. Boulieau's deposition has been lost, but we can lay Mechin's before the reader, for the original has been preserved, just as it issued from his pen:

"I, Gervais Mechin, curate-in-charge of the Church of Saint-Pierre in the Market Place at Loudun, certify by these presents, signed by my hand, to relieve my conscience as to a certain report which is being spread abroad, that I had said in support of an accusation brought by Gilles Robert, archpriest, against Urbain Grandier, priest-in-charge of Saint-Pierre, that I had found the said Grandier lying with women and girls in the church of Saint Pierre, the doors being closed.

"ITEM, that on several different occasions, at unsuitable hours both day and night, I had seen women and girls disturb the said Grandier by going into his bedroom, and that some of the said women remained with him from one o'clock in the after noon till three o'clock the next morning, their maids bringing them their suppers and going away again at once.

"ITEM, that I had seen the said Grandier in the church, the doors being open, but that as soon as some women entered he closed them.

As I earnestly desire that such reports should cease, I declare by these presents that I have never seen the said Grandier with women or girls in the church, the doors being closed; that I have never found him there alone with women or girls; that when he spoke to either someone else was always present, and the doors were open; and as to their posture, I think I made it sufficiently clear when in the witness-box that Grandier was seated and the women scattered over the church; furthermore, I have never seen either women or girls enter Grandier's bedroom either by day or night, although it is true that I have heard people in the corridor coming and going late in the evening, who they were I cannot say, but a brother of the said Grandier sleeps close by; neither have I any knowledge that either women or girls, had their suppers brought to the said room. I have also never said that he neglected the reading of his breviary, because that would be contrary to the truth, seeing that on several occasions he borrowed mine and read his hours in it. I also declare that I have never seen him close the doors of the church, and that whenever I have seen him speaking to women I have never noticed any impropriety; I have not ever seen him touch them in any way, they have only spoken together; and if anything is found in my deposition contrary to the above, it is without my knowledge, and was never read to me, for I would not have signed it, and I say and affirm all this in homage to the truth.

"Done the last day of October 1630, "(Signed) G. MECHIN."

In the face of such proofs of innocence none of the accusations could be considered as established and so, according to the decision of the presidial court of Poitiers, dated the 25th of May 1634, the decision of the bishop's court was reversed, and Grandier was acquitted of the charges brought against him. However, he had still to appear before the Archbishop of Bordeaux, that his acquittal might be ratified. Grandier took advantage of a visit which the archbishop paid to his abbey at Saint-Jouin-les-Marmes, which was only three leagues from Loudun, to make this appearance; his adversaries, who were discouraged by the result of the proceedings at Poitiers, scarcely made any defence, and the archbishop, after an examination which brought clearly to light the innocence of the accused, acquitted and absolved him.

The rehabilitation of Grandier before his bishop had two important results: the first was that it clearly established his innocence, and the second that it brought into prominence his high attainments and eminent qualities. The archbishop seeing the persecutions to which he was subjected, felt a kindly interest in him, and advised him to exchange into some other diocese, leaving a town the principal inhabitants of which appeared to have vowed him a relentless hate.

But such an abandonment of his rights was foreign to the character of Urbain, and he declared to his superior that, strong in His Grace's approbation and the testimony of his own conscience, he would remain in the place to which God had called him. Monseigneur de Sourdis did not feel it his duty to urge Urbain any further, but he had enough insight into his character to perceive that if Urbain should one day fall, it would be, like Satan, through pride; for he added another sentence to his decision, recommending him to fulfil the duties of his office with discretion and modesty, according to the decrees of the Fathers and the canonical constitutions. The triumphal entry of Urbain into Loudun with which we began our narrative shows the spirit in which he took his recommendation.

Chapter II

Urbain Granadier was not satisfied with the arrogant demonstration by which he signalised his return, which even his friends had felt to be ill advised; instead of allowing the hate he had aroused to die away or at least to fall asleep by letting the past be past, he continued with more zeal than ever his proceedings against Duthibaut, and succeeded in obtaining a decree from the Parliament of La Tournelle, by which Duthibaut was summoned before it, and obliged to listen bareheaded to a reprimand, to offer apologies, and to pay damages and costs.

Having thus got the better of one enemy, Urbain turned on the others, and showed himself more indefatigable in the pursuit of justice than they had been in the pursuit of vengeance. The decision of the archbishop had given him a right to a sum of money for compensation, and interest thereon, as well as to the restitution of the revenues of his livings, and there being some demur made, he announced publicly that he intended to exact this reparation to the uttermost farthing, and set about collecting all the evidence which was necessary for the success of a new lawsuit for libel and forgery which he intended to begin. It was in vain that his friends assured him that the vindication of his innocence had been complete and brilliant, it was in vain that they tried to convince him of the danger of driving the vanquished to despair, Urbain replied that he was ready to endure all the persecutions which his enemies might succeed in inflicting on him, but as long as he felt that he had right upon his side he was incapable of drawing back.

Grandier's adversaries soon became conscious of the storm which was gathering above their heads, and feeling that the struggle between themselves and this man would be one of life or death, Mignon, Barot, Meunier, Duthibaut, and Menuau met Trinquant at the village of Pindadane, in a house belonging to the latter, in order to consult about the dangers which threatened them. Mignon had, however, already begun to weave the threads of a new intrigue, which he explained in full to the others; they lent a favourable ear, and his plan was adopted. We shall see it unfold itself by degrees, for it is the basis of our narrative.

We have already said that Mignon was the director of the convent of Ursulines at Loudun: Now the Ursuline order was quite modern, for the historic controversies to which the slightest mention of the martyrdom of St. Ursula and her eleven thousand virgins gave rise, had long hindered the foundation of an order in the saint's honour. However, in 1560 Madame Angele de Bresse established such an order in Italy, with the same rules as the Augustinian order. This gained the approbation of Pope Gregory XIII in 1572. In 1614, Madeleine Lhuillier, with the approval of Pope Paul V, introduced this order into France, by founding a convent at Paris, whence it rapidly spread over the whole kingdom, so-that in 1626, only six years before the time when the events just related took place, a sisterhood was founded in the little town of Loudun.

Although this community at first consisted entirely of ladies of good family, daughters of nobles, officers, judges, and the better class of citizens, and numbered amongst its founders Jeanne de Belfield, daughter of the late Marquis of Cose, and relative of M. de Laubardemont, Mademoiselle de Fazili, cousin of the cardinal-duke, two ladies of the house of Barbenis de Nogaret, Madame de Lamothe, daughter of the Marquis Lamothe-Barace of Anjou, and Madame d'Escoubleau de Sourdis, of the same family as the Archbishop of Bordeaux, yet as these nuns had almost all entered the convent because of their want of fortune, the community found itself at the time of its establishment richer in blood than in money, and was obliged instead of building to purchase a private house. The owner of this house was a certain Moussaut du Frene, whose brother was a priest. This brother, therefore, naturally became the first director of these godly women. Less than a year after his appointment he died, and the directorship became vacant.

The Ursulines had bought the house in which they lived much below its normal value, for it was regarded as a haunted house by all the town. The landlord had rightly thought that there was no better way of getting rid of the ghosts than to confront them with a religious sisterhood, the members of which, passing their days in fasting and prayer, would be hardly likely to have their nights disturbed by bad spirits; and in truth, during the year which they had already passed in the house, no ghost had ever put in an appearance—a fact which had greatly increased the reputation of the nuns for sanctity.

When their director died, it so happened that the boarders took advantage of the occasion to indulge in some diversion at the expense of the older nuns, who were held in general detestation by the youth of the establishment on account of the rigour with which they enforced the rules of the order. Their plan was to raise once more those spirits which had been, as everyone supposed, permanently relegated to outer darkness. So noises began to be heard on the roof of the house, which resolved themselves into cries and groans; then growing bolder, the spirits entered the attics and garrets, announcing their presence by clanking of chains; at last they became so familiar that they invaded the dormitories, where they dragged the sheets off the sisters and abstracted their clothes.

Great was the terror in the convent, and great the talk in the town, so that the mother superior called her wisest, nuns around her and asked them what, in their opinion, would be the best course to take in the delicate circumstances in which they found themselves. Without a dissentient voice, the conclusion arrived at was, that the late director should be immediately replaced by a man still holier than he, if such a man could be found, and whether because he possessed a reputation for sanctity, or for some other reason, their choice fell on Urbain Grandier. When the offer of the post was brought to him, he answered that he was already responsible for two important charges, and that he therefore had not enough time to watch over the snow-white flock which they wished to entrust to him, as a good shepherd should, and he recommended the lady superior to seek out another more worthy and less occupied than himself.

This answer, as may be supposed, wounded the self-esteem of the sisters: they next turned their eyes towards Mignon, priest and canon of the collegiate church of Sainte-Croix, and he, although he felt deeply hurt that they had not thought first of him, accepted the position eagerly; but the recollection that Grandier had been preferred before himself kept awake in, him one of those bitter hatreds which time, instead of soothing, intensifies. From the foregoing narrative the reader can see to what this hate led.

As soon as the new director was appointed, the mother superior confided to him the kind of foes which he would be expected to vanquish. Instead of comforting her by the assurance that no ghosts existing, it could not be ghosts who ran riot in the house, Mignon saw that by pretending to lay these phantoms he could acquire the reputation for holiness he so much desired. So he answered that the Holy Scriptures recognised the existence of ghosts by relating how the witch of Endor had made the shade of Samuel appear to Saul. He went on to say that the ritual of the Church possessed means of driving away all evil spirits, no matter how persistent they were, provided that he who undertook the task were pure in thought and deed, and that he hoped soon, by the help of God, to rid the convent of its nocturnal visitants, whereupon as a preparation for their expulsion he ordered a three days' fast, to be followed by a general confession.

It does not require any great cleverness to understand how easily Mignon arrived at the truth by questioning the young penitents as they came before him. The boarders who had played at being ghosts confessed their folly, saying that they had been helped by a young novice of sixteen years of age, named Marie Aubin. She acknowledged that this was true; it was she who used to get up in the middle of the night, and open the dormitory door, which her more timid room- mates locked most carefully from within every night, before going to bed—a fact which greatly increased their terror when, despite their precautions, the ghosts still got in. Under pretext of not exposing them to the anger of the superior, whose suspicions would be sure to be awakened if the apparitions were to disappear immediately after the general confession, Mignon directed them to renew their nightly frolics from time to time, but at longer and longer intervals. He then sought an interview with the superior, and assured her that he had found the minds of all those under her charge so chaste and pure that he felt sure through his earnest prayers he would soon clear the convent of the spirits which now pervaded it.

Everything happened as the director had foretold, and the reputation for sanctity of the holy man, who by watching and praying had delivered the worthy Ursulines from their ghostly assailants, increased enormously in the town of Loudun.

Chapter III

Hardly had tranquillity been restored when Mignon, Duthibaut, Menuau, Meunier, and Barot, having lost their cause before the Archbishop of Bordeaux, and finding themselves threatened by Grandier with a prosecution for libel and forgery, met together to consult as to the best means of defending themselves before the unbending severity of this man, who would, they felt, destroy them if they did not destroy him.

The result of this consultation was that very shortly afterwards queer reports began to fly about; it was whispered that the ghosts whom the pious director had expelled had again invaded the convent, under an invisible and impalpable form, and that several of the nuns had given, by their words and acts, incontrovertible proofs of being possessed.

When these reports were mentioned to Mignon, he, instead of denying their truth, cast up his eyes to heaven and said that God was certainly a great and merciful God, but it was also certain that Satan was very clever, especially when he was barked by that false human science called magic. However, as to the reports, though they were not entirely without foundation, he would not go so far as to say that any of the sisters were really possessed by devils, that being a question which time alone could decide.

The effect of such an answer on minds already prepared to listen to the most impossible things, may easily be guessed. Mignon let the gossip go its rounds for several months without giving it any fresh food, but at length, when the time was ripe, he called on the priest of Saint-Jacques at Chinon, and told him that matters had now come to such a pass in the Ursuline convent that he felt it impossible to bear up alone under the responsibility of caring for the salvation of the afflicted nuns, and he begged him to accompany him to the convent. This priest, whose name was Pierre Barre, was exactly the man whom Mignon needed in such a crisis. He was of melancholy temperament, and dreamed dreams and saw visions; his one ambition was to gain a reputation for asceticism and holiness. Desiring to surround his visit with the solemnity befitting such an important event, he set out for Loudun at the head of all his parishioners, the whole procession going on foot, in order to arouse interest and curiosity; but this measure was quite needless it took less than that to set the town agog.

While the faithful filled the churches offering up prayers for the success of the exorcisms, Mignon and Barre entered upon their task at the convent, where they remained shut up with the nuns for six hours. At the end of this time Barre appeared and announced to his parishioners that they might go back to Chinon without him, for he had made up his mind to remain for the present at Loudun, in order to aid the venerable director of the Ursuline convent in the holy work he had undertaken; he enjoined on them to pray morning and evening, with all possible fervour, that, in spite of the serious dangers by which it was surrounded, the good cause might finally triumph. This advice, unaccompanied as it was by any explanation, redoubled the curiosity of the people, and the belief gained ground that it was not merely one or two nuns who were possessed of devils, but the whole sisterhood. It was not very long before the name of the magician who had worked this wonder began to be mentioned quite openly: Satan, it was said, had drawn Urbain Grandier into his power, through his pride. Urbain had entered into a pact with the Evil Spirit by which he had sold him his soul in return for being made the most learned man on earth. Now, as Urbain's knowledge was much greater than that of the inhabitants of Loudun, this story gained general credence in the town. although here and there was to be found a man sufficiently enlightened to shrug his shoulders at these absurdities, and to laugh at the mummeries, of which as yet he saw only the ridiculous side,

For the next ten or twelve days Mignon and Barre spent the greater part of their time at the convent; sometimes remaining there for six hours at a stretch, sometimes the entire day. At length, on Monday, the 11th of October, 1632, they wrote to the priest of Venier, to Messire Guillaume Cerisay de la Gueriniere, bailiff of the Loudenois, and to Messire Louis Chauvet, civil lieutenant, begging them to visit the Ursuline convent, in order to examine two nuns who were possessed by evil spirits, and to verify the strange and almost incredible manifestations of this possession. Being thus formally appealed to, the two magistrates could not avoid compliance with the request. It must be confessed that they were not free from curiosity, and felt far from sorry at being able to get to the bottom of the mystery of which for some time the whole town was talking. They repaired, therefore, to the convent, intending to make a thorough investigation as to the reality of the possession and as to the efficacy of the exorcisms employed. Should they judge that the nuns were really possessed, and that those who tried to deliver them were in earnest, they would authorise the continuation of the efforts at exorcism; but if they were not satisfied on these two points, they would soon put an end to the whole thing as a comedy. When they reached the door, Mignon, wearing alb and stole, came to meet them. He told them that the feelings of the nuns had for more than two weeks been harrowed by the apparition of spectres and other blood-curdling visions, that the mother superior and two nuns had evidently been possessed by evil spirits for over a week; that owing to the efforts of Barre and same Carmelite friars who were good enough to assist him against their common enemies, the devils had been temporarily driven out, but on the previous Sunday night, the 10th of October, the mother superior, Jeanne de Belfield, whose conventual name was Jeanne des Anges, and a lay sister called Jeanne Dumagnoux, had again been entered into by the same spirits. It had, however, been discovered by means of exorcisms that a new compact, of which the symbol and token was a bunch of roses, had been concluded, the symbol and token of the first having been three black thorns. He added that during the time of the first possession the demons had refused to give their names, but by the power of his exorcisms this reluctance had been overcome, the spirit which had resumed possession of the mother superior having at length revealed that its name was Ashtaroth, one of the greatest enemies of God, while the devil which had entered into the lay sister was of a lower order, and was called Sabulon. Unfortunately, continued Mignon, just now the two afflicted nuns were resting, and he requested the bailiff and the civil lieutenant to put off their inspection till a little later. The two magistrates were just about to go away, when a nun appeared, saying that the devils were again doing their worst with the two into whom they had entered. Consequently, they accompanied Mignon and the priest from Venier to an upper room, in which were seven narrow beds, of which two only were occupied, one by the mother superior and the other by the lay sister. The superior, who was the more thoroughly possessed of the two, was surrounded by the Carmelite monks, the sisters belonging to the convent, Mathurin Rousseau, priest and canon of Sainte-Croix, and Mannouri, a surgeon from the town.

No sooner did the two magistrates join the others than the superior was seized with violent convulsions, writhing and uttering squeals in exact imitation of a sucking pig. The two magistrates looked on in profound astonishment, which was greatly increased when they saw the patient now bury herself in her bed, now spring right out of it, the whole performance being accompanied by such diabolical gestures and grimaces that, if they were not quite convinced that the possession was genuine, they were at least filled with admiration of the manner in which it was simulated. Mignon next informed the bailiff and the civil lieutenant, that although the superior had never learned Latin she would reply in that language to all the questions addressed to her, if such were their desire. The magistrates answered that as they were there in order to examine thoroughly into the facts of the case, they begged the exorcists to give them every possible proof that the possession was real. Upon this, Mignon approached the mother superior, and, having ordered everyone to be silent, placed two of his fingers in her mouth, and, having gone through the form of exorcism prescribed by the ritual, he asked the following questions word for word as they are given,

>   D. Why have you entered into the body of this young girl?
>   R. Causa animositatis.   —   Out of enmity.
>   D. Per quod pactum ?   —   By what pact?
>   R. Per flores.   —   By flowers.
>   D. Quales?   —   What flowers?
>   R. Rosas.   —   Roses.
>   D. Quis misfit?   —   By whom wert thou sent?

At this question the magistrates remarked that the superior hesitated to reply; twice she opened her mouth in vain, but the third time she said in a weak voice

  D. Dic cognomen? — What is his surname?
  R. Urbanus. — Urbain.

Here there was again the same hesitation, but as if impelled by the will of the exorcist she answered—

  R. Grandier. — Grandier.
  D. Dic qualitatem? — What is his profession?
  R. Sacerdos. — A priest.
  D. Cujus ecclesiae? — Of what church?
  R. Sancti Petri. — Saint-Pierre.
  D. Quae persona attulit flores? — Who brought the flowers?
  R. Diabolica. — Someone sent by the devil.

As the patient pronounced the last word she recovered her senses, and having repeated a prayer, attempted to swallow a morsel of bread which was offered her; she was, however, obliged to spit it out, saying it was so dry she could not get it down.

Something more liquid was then brought, but even of that she could swallow very little, as she fell into convulsions every few minutes.

Upon this the two officials, seeing there was nothing more to be got out of the superior, withdrew to one of the window recesses and began to converse in a low tone; whereupon Mignon, who feared that they had not been sufficiently impressed, followed them, and drew their attention to the fact that there was much in what they had just seen to recall the case of Gaufredi, who had been put to death a few years before in consequence of a decree of the Parliament of Aix, in Provence. This ill-judged remark of Mignon showed so clearly what his aim was that the magistrates made no reply. The civil lieutenant remarked that he had been surprised that Mignon had not made any attempt to find out the cause of the enmity of which the superior had spoken, and which it was so important to find out; but

Mignon excused himself by saying that he had no right to put questions merely to gratify curiosity. The civil lieutenant was about to insist on the matter being investigated, when the lay sister in her turn went into a fit, thus extricating Mignon from his embarrassment. The magistrates approached the lay sister's bed at once, and directed Mignon to put the same questions to her as to the superior: he did so, but all in vain; all she would reply was, "To the other! To the other!"

Mignon explained this refusal to answer by saying that the evil spirit which was in her was of an inferior order, and referred all questioners to Ashtaroth, who was his superior. As this was the only explanation, good or bad, offered them by Mignon, the magistrates went away, and drew up a report of all they had seen and heard without comment, merely appending their signatures.

But in the town very few people showed the same discretion and reticence as the magistrates. The bigoted believed, the hypocrites pretended to believe; and the worldly-minded, who were numerous, discussed the doctrine of possession in all its phases, and made no secret of their own entire incredulity. They wondered, and not without reason it must be confessed, what had induced the devils to go out of the nuns' bodies for two days only, and then come back and resume possession, to the confusion of the exorcists; further, they wanted to know why the mother superior's devil spoke Latin, while the lay sister's was ignorant of that tongue; for a mere difference of rank in the hierarchy of hell did not seem a sufficient explanation of such a difference in education; Mignon's refusal to go on with his interrogations as to the cause of the enmity made them, they said, suspect that, knowing he had reached the end of Ashtaroth's classical knowledge, he felt it useless to try to continue the dialogue in the Ciceronian idiom. Moreover, it was well known that only a few days before all Urbain's worst enemies had met in conclave in the village of Puidardane; and besides, how stupidly Mignon had shown his hand by mentioning Gaufredi, the priest who had been executed at Aix: lastly, why had not a desire for impartiality been shown by calling in other than Carmelite monks to be present at the exorcism, that order having a private quarrel with

Urbain Grandier

Grandier? It must be admitted that this way of looking at the case was not wanting in shrewdness.

On the following day, October 12th, the bailiff and the civil lieutenant, having heard that exorcisms had been again tried without their having been informed beforehand, requested a certain Canon Rousseau to accompany them, and set out with him and their clerk for the convent. On arriving, they asked for Mignon, and on his appearance they told him that this matter of exorcism was of such importance that no further steps were to be taken in it without the authorities being present, and that in future they were to be given timely notice of every attempt to get rid of the evil spirits. They added that this was all the more necessary as Mignon's position as director of the sisterhood and his well-known hate for Grandier would draw suspicions on him unworthy of his cloth, suspicions which he ought to be the first to wish to see dissipated, and that quickly; and that, therefore, the work which he had so piously begun would be completed by exorcists appointed by the court.

Mignon replied that, though he had not the slightest objection to the magistrates being present at all the exorcisms, yet he could not promise that the spirits would reply to anyone except himself and Barre. Just at that moment Barre came on the scene, paler and more gloomy than ever, and speaking with the air of a man whose word no one could help believing, he announced that before their arrival some most extraordinary things had taken place. The magistrates asked what things, and Barre replied that he had learned from the mother superior that she was possessed, not by one, but by seven devils, of whom Ashtaroth was the chief; that Grandier had entrusted his pact with the devil, under the symbol of a bunch of roses, to a certain Jean Pivart, to give to a girl who had introduced it into the convent garden by throwing it over the wall; that this took place in the night between Saturday and Sunday "hora secunda nocturna" (two hours after midnight); that those were the very words the superior had used, but that while she readily named Pivart, she absolutely refused to give the name of the girl; that on asking what Pivart was; she had replied, "Pauper magus" (a poor magician); that he then had pressed her as to the word magus, and that she had replied "Magicianus et civis" (magician and citizen); and that just as she said those words the magistrates had arrived, and he had asked no more questions.

The two officials listened to this information with the seriousness befitting men entrusted with high judicial functions, and announced to the two priests that they proposed to visit the possessed women and witness for themselves the miracles that were taking place. The clerics offered no opposition, but said they feared that the devils were fatigued and would refuse to reply; and, in fact, when the officials reached the sickroom the two patients appeared to have regained some degree of calm. Mignon took advantage of this quiet moment to say mass, to which the two magistrates listened devoutly and tranquilly, and while the sacrifice was being offered the demons did not dare to move. It was expected that they would offer some opposition at the elevation of the Host, but everything passed off without disturbance, only the lay sister's hands and feet twitched a great deal; and this was the only fact which the magistrates thought worthy of mention in their report for that morning. Barre assured them, however, that if they would return about three o'clock the devils would probably have recovered sufficiently from their fatigue to give a second performance.

As the two gentlemen had determined to see the affair to the end, they returned to the convent at the hour named, accompanied by Messire Irenee de Sainte-Marthe, sieur Deshurneaux; and found the room in which the possessed were lying full of curious spectators; for the exorcists had been true prophets—the devils were at work again.

The superior, as always, was the more tormented of the two, as was only to be expected, she having seven devils in her all at once; she was terribly convulsed, and was writhing and foaming at the mouth as if she were mad. No one could long continue in such a condition without serious injury to health; Barre therefore asked the devil-in-chief how soon he would come out. "Cras mane" (To-morrow morning), he replied. The exorcist then tried to hurry him, asking him why he would not come out at once; whereupon the superior murmured the word "Pactum" (A pact); and then "Sacerdos" (A priest), and finally "Finis," or "Finit," for even those nearest could not catch the word distinctly, as the devil, afraid doubtless of perpetrating a barbarism, spoke through the nun's closely clenched teeth. This being all decidedly unsatisfying, the magistrates insisted that the examination should continue, but the devils had again exhausted themselves, and refused to utter another word. The priest even tried touching the superior's head with the pyx, while prayers and litanies were recited, but it was all in vain, except that some of the spectators thought that the contortions of the patient became more violent when the intercessions of certain saints were invoked, as for instance Saints Augustine Jerome, Antony, and Mary Magdalene. Barre next directed the mother superior to dedicate her heart and soul to God, which she did without difficulty; but when he commanded her to dedicate her body also, the chief devil indicated by fresh convulsions that he was not going to allow himself to be deprived of a domicile without resistance, and made those who had heard him say that he would leave the next morning feel that he had only said so under compulsion; and their curiosity as to the result became heightened. At length, however, despite the obstinate resistance of the demon, the superior succeeded in dedicating her body also to God, and thus victorious her features resumed their usual expression, and smiling as if nothing had happened, she turned to Barre and said that there was no vestige of Satan left in her. The civil lieutenant then asked her if she remembered the questions she had been asked and the answers she had given, but she replied that she remembered nothing; but afterwards, having taken some refreshment, she said to those around her that she recollected perfectly how the first possession, over which Mignon had triumphed, had taken place: one evening about ten o'clock, while several nuns were still in her room, although she was already in bed, it seemed to her that someone took her hand and laid something in it, closing her fingers; at that instant she felt a sharp pain as if she had been pricked by three pins, and hearing her scream, the nuns came to her bedside to ask what ailed her. She held out her hand, and they found three black thorns sticking in it, each having made a tiny wound. Just as she had told this tale, the lay sister, as if to prevent all commentary, was seized with convulsions, and Barre recommenced his prayers and exorcisms, but was soon interrupted by shrieks; for one of the persons present had seen a black cat come down the chimney and disappear. Instantly everyone concluded it must be the devil, and began to seek it out. It was not without great difficulty that it was caught; for, terrified at the sight of so many people and at the noise, the poor animal had sought refuge under a canopy; but at last it was secured and carried to the superior's bedside, where Barre began his exorcisms once more, covering the cat with signs of the cross, and adjuring the devil to take his true shape. Suddenly the 'touriere', (the woman who received the tradespeople,) came forward, declaring the supposed devil to be only her cat, and she immediately took possession of it, lest some harm should happen to it.

The gathering had been just about to separate, but Barry fearing that the incident of the cat might throw a ridiculous light upon the evil spirits, resolved to awake once more a salutary terror by announcing that he was going to burn the flowers through which the second spell had been made to work. Producing a bunch of white roses, already faded, he ordered a lighted brazier to be brought. He then threw the flowers on the glowing charcoal, and to the general astonishment they were consumed without any visible effect: the heavens still smiled, no peal of thunder was heard, and no unpleasant odour diffused itself through the room. Barre feeling that the baldness of this act of destruction had had a bad effect, predicted that the morrow would bring forth wondrous things; that the chief devil would speak more distinctly than hitherto; that he would leave the body of the superior, giving such clear signs of his passage that no one would dare to doubt any longer that it was a case of genuine possession. Thereupon the criminal lieutenant, Henri Herve, who had been present during the exorcism, said they must seize upon the moment of his exit to ask about Pivart, who was unknown at Loudun, although everyone who lived there knew everybody else. Barre replied in Latin, "Et hoc dicet epuellam nominabit" (He will not only tell about him, but he will also name the young girl). The young girl whom the devil was to name was, it may be recollected, she who had introduced the flowers into the convent, and whose name the demon until now had absolutely refused to give. On the strength of these promises everyone went home to await the morrow with impatience.

Chapter IV

That evening Grandier asked the bailiff for an audience. At first he had made fun of the exorcisms, for the story had been so badly concocted, and the accusations were so glaringly improbable, that he had not felt the least anxiety. But as the case went on it assumed such an important aspect, and the hatred displayed by his enemies was so intense, that the fate of the priest Gaufredi, referred to by Mignon, occurred to Urbain's mind, and in order to be beforehand with his enemies he determined to lodge a complaint against them. This complaint was founded on the fact that Mignon had performed the rite of exorcism in the presence of the civil lieutenant, the bailiff, and many other persons, and had caused the nuns who were said to be possessed, in the hearing of all these people, to name him, Urbain, as the author of their possession. This being a falsehood and an attack upon his honour, he begged the bailiff, in whose hands the conduct of the affair had been specially placed, to order the nuns to be sequestered, apart from the rest of the sisterhood and from each other, and then to have each separately examined. Should there appear to be any evidence of possession, he hoped that the bailiff would be pleased to appoint clerics of well-known rank and upright character to perform whatever exorcisms were needful; such men having no bias against him would be more impartial than Mignon and his adherents. He also called upon the bailiff to have an exact report drawn up of everything that took place at the exorcisms, in order that, if necessary, he as petitioner might be able to lay it before anyone to whose judgment he might appeal. The bailiff gave Grandier a statement of the conclusions at which he had arrived, and told him that the exorcisms had been performed that day by Barre, armed with the authority of the Bishop of Poitiers himself. Being, as we have seen, a man of common sense and entirely unprejudiced in the matter, the bailiff advised Grandier to lay his complaint before his bishop; but unfortunately he was under the authority of the Bishop of Poitiers, who was so prejudiced against him that he had done everything in his power to induce the Archbishop of Bordeaux to refuse to ratify the decision in favour of Grandier, pronounced by the presidial court. Urbain could not hide from the magistrate that he had nothing to hope for from this quarter, and it was decided that he should wait and see what the morrow would bring forth, before taking any further step.

The impatiently expected day dawned at last, and at eight o'clock in the morning the bailiff, the king's attorney, the civil lieutenant, the criminal lieutenant, and the provost's lieutenant, with their respective clerks, were already at the convent. They found the outer gate open, but the inner door shut. In a few moments Mignon came to them and brought them into a waiting-room. There he told them that the nuns were preparing for communion, and that he would be very much obliged to them if they would withdraw and wait in a house across the street, just opposite the convent, and that he would send them word when they could come back. The magistrates, having first informed Mignon of Urbain's petition, retired as requested.

An hour passed, and as Mignon did not summon them, in spite of his promise, they all went together to the convent chapel, where they were told the exorcisms were already over. The nuns had quitted the choir, and Mignon and Barre came to the grating and told them that they had just completed the rite, and that, thanks to their conjurations, the two afflicted ones were now quite free from evil spirits. They went on to say that they had been working together at the exorcism from seven o'clock in the morning, and that great wonders, of which they had drawn up an account, had come to pass; but they had considered it would not be proper to allow any one else to be present during the ceremony besides the exorcists and the possessed. The bailiff pointed out that their manner of proceedings was not only illegal, but that it laid them under suspicion of fraud and collusion, in the eyes of the impartial: Moreover, as the superior had accused Grandier publicly, she was bound to renew and prove her accusation also publicly, and not in secret; furthermore, it was a great piece of insolence on the part of the exorcists to invite people of their standing and character to come to the convent, and having kept them waiting an hour, to tell them that they considered them unworthy to be admitted to the ceremony which they. had been requested to attend; and he wound up by saying that he would draw up a report, as he had already done on each of the preceding days, setting forth the extraordinary discrepancy between their promises and their performance. Mignon replied that he and Barre had had only one thing in view, viz. the expulsion of the, demons, and that in that they had succeeded, and that their success would be of great benefit to the holy Catholic faith, for they had got the demons so thoroughly into their power that they had been able to command them to produce within a week miraculous proofs of the spells cast on the nuns by Urbain Grandier and their wonderful deliverance therefrom; so that in future no one would be able to doubt as to the reality of the possession. Thereupon the magistrates drew up a report of all that had happened, and of what Barre and Mignon had said. This was signed by all the officials present, except the criminal lieutenant, who declared that, having perfect confidence in the statements of the exorcists, he was anxious to do nothing to increase the doubting spirit which was unhappily so prevalent among the worldly.

The same day the bailiff secretly warned Urbain of the refusal of the criminal lieutenant to join with the others in signing the report, and almost at the same moment he learned that the cause of his adversaries was strengthened by the adhesion of a certain Messire Rene Memin, seigneur de Silly, and prefect of the town. This gentleman was held in great esteem not only on account of his wealth and the many offices which he filled, but above all on account of his powerful friends, among whom was the cardinal-duke himself, to whom he had formerly been of use when the cardinal was only a prior. The character of the conspiracy had now become so alarming that Grandier felt it was time to oppose it with all his strength. Recalling his conversation with the bailiff the preceding day, during which he had advised him to lay his complaint before the Bishop of Poitiers, he set out, accompanied by a priest of Loudun, named Jean Buron, for the prelate's country house at Dissay. The bishop, anticipating his visit, had already given his orders, and Grandier was met by Dupuis, the intendant of the palace, who, in reply to Grandier's request to see the bishop, told him that his lordship was ill. Urbain next addressed himself to the bishop's chaplain, and begged him to inform the prelate that his object in coming was to lay before him the official reports which the magistrates had drawn up of the events which had taken place at the Ursuline convent, and to lodge a complaint as to the slanders and accusations of which he was the victim. Grandier spoke so urgently that the chaplain could not refuse to carry his message; he returned, however, in a few moments, and told Grandier, in the presence of Dupuis, Buron, and a certain sieur Labrasse, that the bishop advised him to take his case to the royal judges, and that he earnestly hoped he would obtain justice from them. Grandier perceived that the bishop had been warned against him, and felt that he was becoming more and more entangled in the net of conspiracy around him; but he was not a man to flinch before any danger. He therefore returned immediately to Loudun, and went once more to the bailiff, to whom he related all that had happened at Dissay; he then, a second time, made a formal complaint as to the slanders circulated with regard to him, and begged the magistrates to have recourse to the king's courts in the business. He also said that he desired to be placed under the protection of the king and his justice, as the accusations made against him were aimed at his honour and his life. The bailiff hastened to make out a certificate of Urbain's protest, which forbade at the same time the repetition of the slanders or the infliction on Urbain of any injury.

Thanks to this document, a change of parts took place: Mignon, the accuser, became the accused. Feeling that he had powerful support behind him, he had the audacity to appear before the bailiff the same day. He said that he did not acknowledge his jurisdiction, as in what concerned Grandier and himself, they being both priests, they could only be judged by their bishop; he nevertheless protested against the complaint lodged by Grandier, which characterised him as a slanderer, and declared that he was ready to give himself up as a prisoner, in order to show everyone that he did not fear the result of any inquiry. Furthermore, he had taken an oath on the sacred elements the day before, in the presence of his parishioners who had come to mass, that in all he had hitherto done he had been moved, not by hatred of Grandier, but by love of the truth, and by his desire for the triumph of the Catholic faith; and he insisted that the bailiff should give him a certificate of his declaration, and served notice of the same on Grandier that very day.

Chapter V

Since October 13th, the day on which the demons had been expelled, life at the convent seemed to have returned to its usual quiet; but Grandier did not let himself be lulled to sleep by the calm: he knew those with whom he was contending too well to imagine for an instant that he would hear no more of them; and when the bailiff expressed pleasure at this interval of repose, Grandier said that it would not last long, as the nuns were only conning new parts, in order to carry on the drama in a more effective manner than ever. And in fact, on November 22nd, Rene Mannouri, surgeon to the convent, was sent to one of his colleagues, named Gaspard Joubert, to beg him to come, bringing some of the physicians of the town with him, to visit the two sisters, who were again tormented by evil spirits. Mannouri, however, had gone to the wrong man, for Joubert had a frank and loyal character, and hated everything that was underhand. Being determined to take no part in the business, except in a public and judicial manner, he applied at once to the bailiff to know if it was by his orders that he was called in. The bailiff said it was not, and summoned Mannouri before him to ask him by whose authority he had sent for Joubert. Mannouri declared that the 'touriere' had run in a fright to his house, saying that the nuns had never been worse possessed than now, and that the director, Mignon, begged him to come at once to the convent, bringing with him all the doctors he could find.

The bailiff, seeing that fresh plots against Grandier were being formed, sent for him and warned him that Barre had come over from Chinon the day before, and had resumed his exorcisms at the convent, adding that it was currently reported in the town that the mother superior and Sister Claire were again tormented by devils. The news neither astonished nor discouraged Grandier, who replied, with his usual smile of disdain, that it was evident his enemies were hatching new plots against him, and that as he had instituted proceedings against them for the former ones, he would take the same course with regard to these. At the same time, knowing how impartial the bailiff was, he begged him to accompany the doctors and officials to the convent, and to be present at the exorcisms, and should any sign of real possession manifest itself, to sequester the afflicted nuns at once, and cause them to be examined by other persons than Mignon and Barré, whom he had such good cause to distrust.

The bailiff wrote to the king's attorney, who, notwithstanding his bias against Grandier, was forced to see that the conclusions arrived at were correct, and having certified this in writing, he at once sent his clerk to the convent to inquire if the superior were still possessed. In case of an affirmative reply being given, the clerk had instructions to warn Mignon and Barré that they were not to undertake exorcisms unless in presence of the bailiff and of such officials and doctors as he might choose to bring with him, and that they would disobey at their peril; he was also to tell them that Grandier's demands to have the nuns sequestered and other exorcists called in were granted.

Mignon and Barré listened while the clerk read his instructions, and then said they refused to recognise the jurisdiction of the bailiff in this case; that they had been summoned by the mother superior and Sister Claire when their strange illness returned, an illness which they were convinced was nothing else than possession by evil spirits; that they had hitherto carried out their exorcisms under the authority of a commission given them by the Bishop of Poitiers; and as the time for which they had permission had not yet expired; they would continue to exorcise as often as might be necessary. They had, however, given notice to the worthy prelate of what was going on, in order that he might either come himself or send other exorcists as best suited him, so that a valid opinion as to the reality, of the possession might be procured, for up to the present the worldly and unbelieving had taken upon themselves to declare in an off-hand manner that the whole affair was a mixture of fraud and delusion, in contempt of the glory of God and the Catholic religion. As to the rest of the message, they would not, in any way prevent the bailiff and the other officials, with as many medical men as they chose to bring, from seeing the nuns, at least until they heard from the bishop, from whom they expected a letter next day. But it was for the nuns themselves to say whether it was convenient for them to receive visitors; as far as concerned themselves, they desired to renew their protest, and declared they could not accept the bailiff as their judge, and did not think that it could be legal for them to refuse to obey a command from their ecclesiastical superiors, whether with relation to exorcism or any other thing of which the ecclesiastical courts properly took cognisance. The clerk brought this answer to the bailiff, and he, thinking it was better to wait for the arrival of the bishop or of fresh orders from him, put off his visit to the convent until the next day. But the next day came without anything being heard of the prelate himself or of a messenger from him.

Early in the morning the bailiff went to the convent, but was not admitted; he then waited patiently until noon, and seeing that no news had arrived from Dissay, and that the convent gates were still closed against him, he granted a second petition of Grandier's, to the effect that Byre and Mignon should be prohibited from questioning the superior and the other nuns in a manner tending to blacken the character of the petitioner or any other person. Notice of this prohibition was served the same day on Barre and on one nun chosen to represent the community. Barre did not pay the slightest attention to this notice, but kept on asserting that the bailiff had no right to prevent his obeying the commands of his bishop, and declaring that henceforward he would perform all exorcisms solely under ecclesiastical sanction, without any reference to lay persons, whose unbelief and impatience impaired the solemnity with which such rites should be conducted.

The best part of the day having gone over without any sign of either bishop or messenger, Grandier presented a new petition to the bailiff. The bailiff at once summoned all the officers of the bailiwick and the attorneys of the king, in order to lay it before them; but the king's attorneys refused to consider the matter, declaring upon their honour that although they did not accuse Grandier of being the cause, yet they believed that the nuns were veritably possessed, being convinced by the testimony of the devout ecclesiastics in whose presence the evil spirits had come out. This was only the ostensible reason for their refusal, the real one being that the advocate was a relation of Mignon's, and the attorney a son-in-law of Trinquant's, to whose office he had succeeded. Thus Grandier, against whom were all the ecclesiastical judges, began to feel as if he were condemned beforehand by the judges of the royal courts, for he knew how very short was the interval between the recognition of the possession as a fact and the recognition of himself as its author.

Nevertheless, in spite of the formal declarations of the king's advocate and attorney, the bailiff ordered the superior and the lay sister to be removed to houses in town, each to be accompanied by a nun as companion. During their absence from the convent they were to be looked after by exorcists, by women of high character and position, as well as by physicians and attendants, all of whom he himself would appoint, all others being forbidden access to the nuns without his permission.

The clerk was again sent to the convent with a copy of this decision, but the superior having listened to the reading of the document, answered that in her own name and that of the sisterhood she refused to recognise the jurisdiction of the bailiff; that she had already received directions from the Bishop of Poitiers, dated 18th November, explaining the measures which were to be taken in the matter, and she would gladly send a copy of these directions to the bailiff, to prevent his pleading ignorance of them; furthermore, she demurred to the order for her removal, having vowed to live always secluded in a convent, and that no one could dispense her from this vow but the bishop. This protest having been made in the presence of Madame de Charnisay, aunt of two of the nuns, and Surgeon Mannouri, who was related to another, they both united in drawing up a protest against violence, in case the bailiff should insist on having his orders carried out, declaring that, should he make the attempt, they would resist him, as if he were a mere private individual. This document being duly signed and witnessed was immediately sent to the bailiff by the hand of his own clerk, whereupon the bailiff ordered that preparations should be made with regard to the sequestration, and announced that the next day, the 24th November, he would repair to the convent and be present at the exorcisms.

The next day accordingly, at the appointed hour, the bailiff summoned Daniel Roger, Vincent de Faux, Gaspard Joubert, and Matthieu Fanson, all four physicians, to his presence, and acquainting them with his reasons for having called them, asked them to accompany him to the convent to examine, with the most scrupulous impartiality, two nuns whom he would point out, in order to discover if their illness were feigned, or arose from natural or supernatural causes. Having thus instructed them as to his wishes, they all set out for the convent.

They were shown into the chapel and placed close to the altar, being separated by a grating from the choir, in which the nuns who sang usually sat. In a few moments the superior was carried in on a small bed, which was laid down before the grating. Barre then said mass, during which the superior went into violent convulsions. She threw her arms about, her fingers were clenched, her cheeks enormously inflated, and her eyes turned up so that only the whites could be seen.

The mass finished, Barre approached her to administer the holy communion and to commence the exorcism. Holding the holy wafer in his hand, he said —

"Adora Deum tuum, creatorem tuum" (Adore God, thy Creator).

The superior hesitated, as if she found great difficulty in making this act of love, but at length she said —

"Adoro te" (I adore Thee).

"Quem adoras?" (Whom dost thou adore?)

"Jesus Christus" (Jesus Christ), answered the nun, quite unconscious that the verb adorn governs accusative.

This mistake, which no sixth-form boy would make, gave rise to bursts of laughter in the church; and Daniel Douin, the provost's assessor, was constrained to say aloud —

"There's a devil for you, who does not know much about transitive verbs."

Barre perceiving the bad impression that the superior's nominative had made, hastened to ask her—

"Quis est iste quem adoras?" (Who is it whom thou dost adore?)

His hope was that she would again reply " Jesus Christus," but he was disappointed.

"Jesu Christe," was her answer.

Renewed shouts of laughter greeted this infraction of one of the most elementary rules of syntax, and several of those present exclaimed

"Oh, your reverence, what very poor Latin!"

Barre pretended not to hear, and next asked what was the name of the demon who had taken possession of her. The poor superior, who was greatly confused by the unexpected effect of her last two answers, could not speak for a long time; but at length with great trouble she brought out the name Asmodee, without daring to latinise it. The exorcist then inquired how many devils the superior had in her body, and to this question she replied quite fluently

"Sex" (Six).

The bailiff upon this requested Barre to ask the chief devil how many evil spirits he had with him. But the need for this answer had been foreseen, and the nun unhesitatingly returned

"Quinque" (Five).

This answer raised Asmodee somewhat in the opinion of those present; but when the bailiff adjured the superior to repeat in Greek what she had just said in Latin she made no reply, and on the adjuration being renewed she immediately recovered her senses.

The examination of the superior being thus cut short, a little nun who appeared for the first time in public was brought forward. She began by twice pronouncing the name of Grandier with a loud laugh; then turning to the bystanders, called out—

"For all your number, you can do nothing worth while."

As it was easy to see that nothing of importance was to be expected from this new patient, she was soon suppressed, and her place taken by the lay sister Claire who had already made her debut in the mother superior's room

Hardly had she entered the choir than she uttered a groan, but as soon as they placed her on the little bed on which the other nuns had lain, she gave way to uncontrollable laughter, and cried out between the paroxysms

"Grandier, Grandier, you must buy some at the market."

Barre at once declared that these wild and whirling words were a proof of possession, and approached to exorcise the demon; but Sister Claire resisted, and pretending to spit in the face of the exorcist, put out her tongue at him, making indecent gestures, using a word in harmony with her actions. This word being in the vernacular was understood by everyone and required no interpretation.

The exorcist then conjured her to give the name of the demon who was in her, and she replied

"Grandier."

But Barre by repeating his question gave her to understand that she had made a mistake, whereupon she corrected herself and said

"Elimi."

Nothing in the world could induce her to reveal the number of evil spirits by whom Elimi was accompanied, so that Barre, seeing that it was useless to press her on this point, passed on to the next question.

"Quo pacto ingressus est daemon"(By what pact did the demon get in?).

"Duplex" (Double), returned Sister Claire.

This horror of the ablative, when the ablative was absolutely necessary, aroused once more the hilarity of the audience, and proved that Sister Claire's devil was just as poor a Latin scholar as the superior's, and Barre, fearing some new linguistic eccentricity on the part of the evil spirit, adjourned the meeting to another day.

The paucity of learning shown in the answers of the nuns being sufficient to convince any fairminded person that the whole affair was a ridiculous comedy, the bailiff felt encouraged to persevere until he had unravelled the whole plot. Consequently, at three o'clock in the afternoon, he returned to the convent, accompanied by his clerk, by several magistrates, and by a considerable number of the best known people of Loudun, and asked to see the superior. Being admitted, he announced to Barre that he had come to insist on the superior being separated from Sister Claire, so that each could be exorcised apart. Barre dared not refuse before such a great number of witnesses, therefore the superior was isolated and the exorcisms begun all over again. Instantly the convulsions returned, just as in the morning, only that now she twisted her feet into the form of hooks, which was a new accomplishment.

Having adjured her several times, the exorcist succeeded in making her repeat some prayers, and then sounded her as to the name and number of the demons in possession, whereupon she said three times that there was one called Achaos. The bailiff then directed Barre to ask if she were possessed 'ex pacto magi, aut ex Aura voluntate Dei' (by a pact with a sorcerer or by the pure will of God), to which the superior answered

"Non est voluutas Dei" (Not by the will of God).

Upon this, Barre dreading more questions from the bystanders, hastily resumed his own catechism by asking who was the sorcerer.

"Urbanus," answered the superior.

"Est-ne Urbanus papa" (Is it Pope Urban?), asked the exorcist.

"Grandier," replied the superior.

"Quare ingressus es in corpus hujus puellae" (Why did you enter the body of this maiden?), said Barre.

"Propter praesentiam tuum" (Because of your presence), answered the superior.

At this point the bailiff, seeing no reason why the dialogue between Barre and the superior should ever come to an end, interposed and demanded that questions suggested by him and the other officials present should be put to the superior, promising that if she answered three of four such questions correctly, he, and those with him, would believe in the reality of the possession, and would certify to that effect. Barre accepted the challenge, but unluckily just at that moment the superior regained consciousness, and as it was already late, everyone retired.

Chapter VI

The next day, November 25th, the bailiff and the majority of the officers of the two jurisdictions came to the convent once more, and were all conducted to the choir. In a few moments the curtains behind the grating were drawn back, and the superior, lying on her bed, came to view. Barre began, as usual, by the celebration of mass, during which the superior was seized with convulsions, and exclaimed two or three times, "Grandier! Grandier! false priest!" When the mass was over, the celebrant went behind the grating, carrying the pyx; then, placing it on his head and holding it there, he protested that in all he was doing he was actuated by the purest motives and the highest integrity; that he had no desire to harm anyone on earth; and he adjured God to strike him dead if he had been guilty of any bad action or collusion, or had instigated the nuns to any deceit during the investigation.

The prior of the Carmelites next advanced and made the same declaration, taking the oath in the same manner, holding the pyx over his head; and further calling down on himself and his brethren the curse of Korah, Dathan, and Abiram if they had sinned during this inquiry. These protestations did not, however, produce the salutary effect intended, some of those present saying aloud that such oaths smacked of sacrilege.

Barre hearing the murmurs, hastened to begin the exorcisms, first advancing to the superior to offer her the holy sacrament: but as soon as she caught sight of him she became terribly convulsed, and attempted to drag the pyx from his hands. Barre, however, by pronouncing the sacred words, overcame the repulsion of the superior, and succeeded in placing the wafer in her mouth; she, however, pushed it out again with her tongue, as if it made her sick; Barge caught it in his fingers and gave it to her again, at the same time forbidding the demon to make her vomit, and this time she succeeded in partly swallowing the sacred morsel, but complained that it stuck in her throat. At last, in order to get it down, Barge three times gave her water to drink; and then, as always during his exorcisms, he began by interrogating the demon.

"Per quod pactum ingressus es in corpus hujus puellae?" (By what pact didst thou enter the body of this maiden?)

"Aqua" (By water), said the superior.

One of those who had accompanied the bailiff was a Scotchman called Stracan, the head of the Reformed College of Loudun. Hearing this answer, he called on the demon to translate aqua into Gaelic, saying if he gave this proof of having those linguistic attainments which all bad spirits possess, he and those with him would be convinced that the possession was genuine and no deception. Barre, without being in the least taken aback, replied that he would make the demon say it if God permitted, and ordered the spirit to answer in Gaelic. But though he repeated his command twice, it was not obeyed; on the third repetition the superior said—

"Nimia curiositas" (Too much curiosity), and on being asked again, said—

"Deus non volo."

This time the poor devil went astray in his conjugation, and confusing the first with the third person, said, "God, I do not wish," which in the context had no meaning. "God does not wish," being the appointed answer.

The Scotchman laughed heartily at this nonsense, and proposed to Barre to let his devil enter into competition with the boys of his seventh form; but Barre, instead of frankly accepting the challenge in the devil's name, hemmed and hawed, and opined that the devil was justified in not satisfying idle curiosity.

"But, sir, you must be aware," said the civil lieutenant, "and if you are not, the manual you hold in your hand will teach you, that the gift of tongues is one of the unfailing symptoms of true possession, and the power to tell what is happening at a distance another."

"Sir," returned Barre, "the devil knows the language very well, but, does not wish to speak it; he also knows all your sins, in proof of which, if you so desire, I shall order him to give the list."

"I shall be delighted to hear it," said the civil lieutenant; "be so good as to try the experiment."

Barre was about to approach the superior, when he was held back by the bailiff, who remonstrated with him on the impropriety of his conduct, whereupon Barre assured the magistrate that he had never really intended to do as he threatened.

However, in spite of all Barre's attempts to distract the attention of the bystanders from the subject, they still persisted in desiring to discover the extent of the devil's knowledge of foreign languages, and at their suggestion the bailiff proposed to Barre to try him in Hebrew instead of Gaelic. Hebrew being, according to Scripture, the most ancient language of all, ought to be familiar to the demon, unless indeed he had forgotten it. This idea met with such general applause that Barre was forced to command the possessed nun to say aqua in Hebrew. The poor woman, who found it difficult enough to repeat correctly the few Latin words she had learned by rote, made an impatient movement, and said—

"I can't help it; I retract" (Je renie).

These words being heard and repeated by those near her produced such an unfavourable impression that one of the Carmelite monks tried to explain them away by declaring that the superior had not said "Je renie," but "Zaquay," a Hebrew word corresponding to the two Latin words, "Effudi aquam" (I threw water about). But the words "Je renie" had been heard so distinctly that the monk's assertion was greeted with jeers, and the sub-prior reprimanded him publicly as a liar. Upon this, the superior had a fresh attack of convulsions, and as all present knew that these attacks usually indicated that the performance was about to end, they withdrew, making very merry over a devil who knew neither Hebrew nor Gaelic, and whose smattering of Latin was so incorrect.

However, as the bailiff and civil lieutenant were determined to clear up every doubt so far as they still felt any, they went once again to the convent at three o'clock the same afternoon. Barre came out to meet them, and took them for a stroll in the convent grounds. During their walk he said to the civil lieutenant that he felt very much surprised that he, who had on a former occasion, by order of the Bishop of Poitiers, laid information against Grandier should be now on his side. The civil lieutenant replied that he would be ready to inform against him again if there were any justification, but at present his object was to arrive at the truth, and in this he felt sure he should be successful. Such an answer was very unsatisfactory to Barre; so, drawing the bailiff aside, he remarked to him that a man among whose ancestors were many persons of condition, several of whom had held positions of much dignity in the Church, and who himself held such an important judicial position, ought to show less incredulity in regard to the possibility of a devil entering into a human body, since if it were proved it would redound to the glory of God and the good of the Church and of religion. The bailiff received this remonstrance with marked coldness, and replied that he hoped always to take justice for his guide, as his duty commanded. Upon this, Barre pursued the subject no farther, but led the way to the superior's apartment.

Just as they entered the room, where a large number of people were already gathered, the superior, catching sight of the pyx which Barre had brought with him, fell once more into convulsions. Barre went towards her, and having asked the demon as usual by what pact he had entered the maiden's body, and received the information that it was by water, continued his examination as follows:

"Quis finis pacti" (What is the object of this pact?

"Impuritas" (Unchastity).

Urbain Grandier

At these words the bailiff interrupted the exorcist and ordered him to make the demon say in Greek the three words, 'finis, pacti, impuritas'. But the superior, who had once already got out of her difficulties by an evasive answer, had again recourse to the same convenient phrase, "Nimia curiositas," with which Barre agreed, saying that they were indeed too much given to curiosity. So the bailiff had to desist from his attempt to make the demon speak Greek, as he had before been obliged to give up trying to make him speak Hebrew and Gaelic. Barre then continued his examination.

"Quis attulit pactum?" (Who brought the pact ?)

"Magus" (The sorcerer).

"Quale nomen magi?" (What is the sorcerer's name?)

"Urbanus" (Urban).

"Quis Urbanus? Est-ne Urbanus papa?"

(What Urban? Pope Urban?)

"Grandier."

"Cujus qualitatis?" (What is his profession?)

"Curcatus."

The enriching of the Latin language by this new and unknown word produced a great effect on the audience; however, Barre did not pause long enough to allow it to be received with all the consideration it deserved, but went on at once.

"Quis attulit aquam pacti?" (Who brought the water of the pact?)

"Magus" (The magician).

"Qua hora?" (At what o'clock?)

"Septima" (At seven o'clock).

"An matutina?" (In the morning?)

"Sego" (In the evening).

"Quomodo intravit?" (How did he enter?)

"Janua" (By the door).

"Quis vidit?" (Who saw him?)

"Tres" (Three persons).

Here Barre stopped, in order to confirm the testimony of the devil, assuring his hearers that the Sunday after the superior's deliverance from the second possession he along with Mignon and one of the sisters was sitting with her at supper, it being about seven o'clock in the evening, when she showed them drops of water on her arm, and no one could tell where they came from. He had instantly washed her arm in holy water and repeated some prayers, and while he was saying them the breviary of the superior was twice dragged from her hands and thrown at his feet, and when he stooped to pick it up for the second time he got a box on the ear without being able to see the hand that administered it. Then Mignon came up and confirmed what Barre had said in a long discourse, which he wound up by calling down upon his head the most terrible penalties if every word he said were not the exact truth. He then dismissed the assembly, promising to drive out the evil spirit the next day, and exhorting those present to prepare themselves, by penitence and receiving the holy communion, for the contemplation of the wonders which awaited them.

Chapter VII

The last two exorcisms had been so much talked about in the town, that Grandier, although he had not been present, knew everything that had happened, down to the smallest detail, so he once more laid a complaint before the bailiff, in which he represented that the nuns maliciously continued to name him during the exorcisms as the author of their pretended possession, being evidently influenced thereto by his enemies, whereas in fact not only had he had no communication with them, but had never set eyes on them; that in order to prove that they acted under influence it was absolutely necessary that they should be sequestered, it being most unjust that Mignon and Barre, his mortal enemies, should have constant access to them and be able to stay with them night and day, their doing so making the collusion evident and undeniable; that the honour of God was involved, and also that of the petitioner, who had some right to be respected, seeing that he was first in rank among the ecclesiastics of the town.

Taking all this into consideration, he consequently prayed the bailiff to be pleased to order that the nuns buffering from the so- called possession should at once be separated from each other and from their present associates, and placed under the control of clerics assisted by physicians in whose impartiality the petitioner could have confidence; and he further prayed that all this should be performed in spite of any opposition or appeal whatsoever (but without prejudice to the right of appeal), because of the importance of the matter. And in case the bailiff were not pleased to order the sequestration, the petitioner would enter a protest and complaint against his refusal as a withholding of justice.

The bailiff wrote at the bottom of the petition that it would be at once complied with.

After Urbain Grandier had departed, the physicians who had been present at the exorcisms presented themselves before the bailiff, bringing their report with them. In this report they said that they had recognised convulsive movements of the mother superior's body, but that one visit was not sufficient to enable them to make a thorough diagnosis, as the movements above mentioned might arise as well from a natural as from supernatural causes; they therefore desired to be afforded opportunity for a thorough examination before being called on to pronounce an opinion. To this end they required permission to spend several days and nights uninterruptedly in the same room with the patients, and to treat them in the presence of other nuns and some of the magistrates. Further, they required that all the food and medicine should pass through the doctors' hands, and that no one, should touch the patients except quite openly, or speak to them except in an audible voice. Under these conditions they would undertake to find out the true cause of the convulsions and to make a report of the same.

It being now nine o'clock in the morning, the hour when the exorcisms began, the bailiff went over at once to the convent, and found Barre half way through the mass, and the superior in convulsions. The magistrate entered the church at the moment of the elevation of the Host, and noticed among the kneeling Catholics a young man called Dessentier standing up with his hat on. He ordered him either to uncover or to go away. At this the convulsive movements of the superior became more violent, and she cried out that there were Huguenots in the church, which gave the demon great power over her. Barre asked her how many there were present, and she replied, "Two," thus proving that the devil was no stronger in arithmetic than in Latin; for besides Dessentier, Councillor Abraham Gauthier, one of his brothers, four of his sisters, Rene Fourneau, a deputy, and an attorney called Angevin, all of the Reformed faith, were present.

As Barre saw that those present were greatly struck, by this numerical inaccuracy, he tried to turn their thoughts in another direction by asking the superior if it were true that she knew no Latin. On her replying that she did not know a single word, he held the pyx before her and ordered her to swear by the holy sacrament. She resisted at first, saying loud enough for those around her to hear—

"My father, you make me take such solemn oaths that I fear God will punish me."

To this Barre replied—

"My daughter, you must swear for the glory of God."

And she took the oath.

Just then one of the bystanders remarked that the mother superior was in the habit of interpreting the Catechism to her scholars. This she denied, but acknowledged that she used to translate the Paternoster and the Creed for them. As the superior felt herself becoming somewhat confused at this long series of embarrassing questions, she decided on going into convulsions again, but with only moderate success, for the bailiff insisted that the exorcists should ask her where Grandier was at that very moment. Now, as the ritual teaches that one of the proofs of possession is the faculty of telling, when asked, where people are, without seeing them, and as the question was propounded in the prescribed terms, she was bound to answer, so she said that Grandier was in the great hall of the castle.

"That is not correct," said the bailiff, "for before coming here I pointed out a house to Grandier and asked him to stay in it till I came back. If anybody will go there, they will be sure to find him, for he wished to help me to discover the truth without my being obliged to resort to sequestration, which is a difficult measure to take with regard to nuns."

Barre was now ordered to send some of the monks present to the castle, accompanied by a magistrate and a clerk. Barre chose the Carmelite prior, and the bailiff Charles Chauvet, assessor of the bailiwick, Ismael Boulieau a priest, and Pierre Thibaut, an articled clerk, who all set out at once to execute their commission, while the rest of those present were to await their return.

Meanwhile the superior, who had not spoken a word since the bailiff's declaration, remained, in spite of repeated exorcisms, dumb, so Barre sent for Sister Claire, saying that one devil would encourage the other. The bailiff entered a formal protest against this step, insisting that the only result of a double exorcism would be to cause confusion, during which suggestions might be conveyed to the superior, and that the proper thing to do was, before beginning new conjurations, to await the return of the messengers. Although the bailiff's suggestion was most reasonable, Barre knew better than to adopt it, for he felt that no matter what it cost he must either get rid of the bailiff and all the other officials who shared his doubts, or find means with the help of Sister Claire to delude them into belief. The lay sister was therefore brought in, in spite of the opposition of the bailiff and the other magistrates, and as they did not wish to seem to countenance a fraud, they all withdrew, declaring that they could no longer look on at such a disgusting comedy. In the courtyard they met their messengers returning, who told them they had gone first to the castle and had searched the great hall and all the other rooms without seeing anything of Grandier; they had then gone to the house mentioned by the bailiff, where they found him for whom they were looking, in the company of Pere Veret, the confessor of the nuns, Mathurin Rousseau, and Nicolas Benoit, canons, and Conte, a doctor, from whom they learned that Grandier had not been an instant out of their sight for the last two hours. This being all the magistrates wanted to know, they went home, while their envoys went upstairs and told their story, which produced the effect which might be expected. Thereupon a Carmelite brother wishing to weaken the impression, and thinking that the devil might be more lucky in his, second guess than the first, asked the superior where Grandier was just then. She answered without the slightest hesitation that he was walking with the bailiff in the church of Sainte-Croix. A new deputation was at once sent off, which finding the church empty, went on to the palace, and saw the bailiff presiding at a court. He had gone direct from the convent to the palace, and had not yet seen Grandier. The same day the nuns sent word that they would not consent to any more exorcisms being performed in the presence of the bailiff and the officials who usually accompanied him, and that for the future they were determined to answer no questions before such witnesses.

Grandier learning of this piece of insolence, which prevented the only man on whose impartiality he could reckon from being henceforward present at the exorcisms, once more handed in a petition to the bailiff, begging for the sequestration of the two nuns, no matter at what risk. The bailiff, however, in the interests of the petitioner himself, did not dare to grant this request, for he was afraid that the ecclesiastical authorities would nullify his procedure, on the ground that the convent was not under his jurisdiction.

He, however, summoned a meeting of the principal inhabitants of the town, in order to consult with them as to the best course to take for the public good. The conclusion they arrived at was to write to the attorney-general and to the Bishop of Poitiers, enclosing copies of the reports which had been drawn up, and imploring them to use their authority to put an end to these pernicious intrigues. This was done, but the attorney-general replied that the matter being entirely ecclesiastical the Parliament was not competent to take cognisance of it. As for the bishop, he sent no answer at all.

He was not, however, so silent towards Grandier's enemies; for the ill-success of the exorcisms of November 26th having made increased precautions necessary, they considered it would be well to apply to the bishop for a new commission, wherein he should appoint certain ecclesiastics to represent him during the exorcisms to come. Barre himself went to Poitiers to make this request. It was immediately granted, and the bishop appointed Bazile, senior-canon of Champigny, and Demorans, senior canon of Thouars, both of whom were related to some of Grandier's adversaries. The following is a copy of the new commission:

> "Henri-Louis le Chataignier de la Rochepezai, by the divine will Bishop of Poitiers, to the senior canons of the Chatelet de Saint-Pierre de Thouars et de Champigny-sur-Vese, greeting:

"We by these presents command you to repair to the town of Loudun, to the convent of the nuns of Sainte-Ursule, to be present at the exorcisms which will be undertaken by Sieur Barre upon some nuns of the said convent who are tormented by evil spirits, we having thereto authorised the said Barre. You are also to draw up a report of all that takes place, and for this purpose are to take any clerk you may choose with you.

" Given and done at Poitiers, November 28th, 1632.

"(Signed) HENRI LOUIS, Bishop of Poitiers.

"(Countersigned) By order of the said Lord Bishop, "MICHELET"

These two commissioners having been notified beforehand, went to Loudun, where Marescot, one of the queen's chaplains, arrived at the same time; for the pious queen, Anne of Austria, had heard so many conflicting accounts of the possession of the Ursuline nuns, that she desired, for her own edification, to get to the bottom of the affair. We can judge what importance the case was beginning to assume by its being already discussed at court.

In spite of the notice which had been sent them that the nuns would not receive them, the bailiff and the civil lieutenant fearing that the royal envoy would allow himself to be imposed on, and would draw up an account which would cast doubt on the facts contained in their reports, betook themselves to the convent on December 1st, the day on which the exorcisms were to recommence, in the presence of the new commissioners. They were accompanied by their assessor, by the provost's lieutenant, and a clerk. They had to knock repeatedly before anyone seemed to hear them, but at length a nun opened the door and told them they could not enter, being suspected of bad faith, as they had publicly declared that the possession was a fraud and an imposture. The bailiff, without wasting his time arguing with the sister, asked to see Barre, who soon appeared arrayed in his priestly vestments, and surrounded by several persons, among whom was the queen's chaplain. The bailiff complained that admittance had been refused to him and those with him, although he had been authorised to visit the convent by the Bishop of Poitiers. Barre' replied that he would not hinder their coming in, as far as it concerned him.

"We are here with the intention of entering," said the bailiff, "and also for the purpose of requesting you to put one or two questions to the demon which we have drawn up in terms which are in accordance with what is prescribed in the ritual. I am sure you will not refuse," he added, turning with a bow to Marescot, "to make this experiment in the presence of the queen's chaplain, since by that means all those suspicions of imposture can be removed which are unfortunately so rife concerning this business."

"In that respect I shall do as I please, and not as you order me," was the insolent reply of the exorcist.

"It is, however, your duty to follow legal methods in your procedure," returned the bailiff, "if you sincerely desire the truth; for it would be an affront to God to perform a spurious miracle in His honour, and a wrong to the Catholic faith, whose power is in its truth, to attempt to give adventitious lustre to its doctrines by the aid of fraud and deception."

"Sir," said Barre, "I am a man of honour, I know my duty and I shall discharge it; but as to yourself, I must recall to your recollection that the last time you were here you left the chapel in anger and excitement, which is an attitude of mind most unbecoming in one whose duty it is to administer justice."

Seeing that these recriminations would have no practical result, the magistrates cut them short by reiterating their demand for admittance; and on this being refused, they reminded the exorcists that they were expressly prohibited from asking any questions tending to cast a slur on the character of any person or persons whatever, under pain of being treated as disturbers of the public peace. At this warning Barre, saying that he did not acknowledge the bailiff's jurisdiction, shut the door in the faces of the two magistrates.

As there was no time to lose if the machinations of his enemies were to be brought to nought, the bailiff and the civil lieutenant advised Grandier to write to the Archbishop of Bordeaux, who had once already extricated him from imminent danger, setting forth at length his present predicament; this letter; accompanied by the reports drawn up by the bailiff and the civil lieutenant, were sent off at once by a trusty messenger to His Grace of Escoubleau de Sourdis. As soon as he received the despatches, the worthy prelate seeing how grave was the crisis, and that the slightest delay might be fatal to Grandier, set out at once for his abbey of Saint-Jouinles-Marmes, the place in which he had already vindicated in so striking a manner the upright character of the poor persecuted priest by a fearless act of justice.

It is not difficult to realise what a blow his arrival was to those who held a brief for the evil spirits in possession; hardly had he reached Saint-Jouin than he sent his own physician to the convent with orders to see the afflicted nuns and to test their condition, in order to judge if the convulsions were real or simulated. The physician arrived, armed with a letter from the archbishop, ordering Mignon to permit the bearer to make a thorough examination into the position of affairs. Mignon received the physician with all the respect due to him who sent him, but expressed great regret that he had not come a little sooner, as, thanks to his (Mignon's) exertions and those of Barre, the devils had been exorcised the preceding day. He nevertheless introduced the archbishop's envoy to the presence of the superior and Sister Claire, whose demeanour was as calm as if they had never been disturbed by any agitating' experiences. Mignon's statement being thus confirmed, the doctor returned to Saint-Jouin, the only thing to which he could bear testimony being the tranquillity which reigned at the moment in the convent.

The imposture being now laid so completely bare, the archbishop was convinced that the infamous persecutions to which it had led would cease at once and for ever; but Grandier, better acquainted with the character of his adversaries, arrived on the 27th of December at the abbey and laid a petition at the archbishop's feet. In this document he set forth that his enemies having formerly brought false and slanderous accusations, against him of which, through the justice of the archbishop, he had been able to clear himself, had employed themselves during the last three months in inventing and publishing as a fact that the petitioner had sent evil spirits into the bodies of nuns in the Ursuline convent of Loudun, although he had never spoken to any of the sisterhood there; that the guardianship of the sisters who, it was alleged, were possessed, and the task of exorcism, had been entrusted to Jean Mignon and Pierre Barre, who had in the most unmistakable manner shown themselves to be the mortal enemies of the petitioner; that in the reports drawn up by the said Jean Mignon and Pierre Barre, which differed so widely from those made by the bailiff and the civil lieutenant, it was boastfully alleged that three or four times devils had been driven out, but that they had succeeded in returning and taking possession of their victims again and again, in virtue of successive pacts entered into between the prince of darkness and the petitioner; that the aim of these reports and allegations was to destroy the reputation of the petitioner and excite public opinion against him; that although the demons had been put to flight by the arrival of His Grace, yet it was too probable that as soon as he was gone they would return to the charge; that if, such being the case, the powerful support of the archbishop were not available, the innocence of the petitioner, no matter how strongly established, would by the cunning tactics of his inveterate foes be obscured and denied: he, the petitioner, therefore prayed that, should the foregoing reasons prove on examination to be cogent, the archbishop would be pleased to prohibit Barre, Mignon, and their partisans, whether among the secular or the regular clergy, from taking part in any future exorcisms, should such be necessary, or in the control of any persons alleged to be possessed; furthermore, petitioner prayed that His Grace would be pleased to appoint as a precautionary measure such other clerics and lay persons as seemed to him suitable, to superintend the administration of food and medicine and the rite of exorcism to those alleged to be possessed, and that all the treatment should be carried out in the presence of magistrates.

The archbishop accepted the petition, and wrote below it:

"The present petition having been seen by us and the opinion of our attorney having been taken in the matter, we have sent the petitioner in advance of our said attorney back to Poitiers, that justice may be done him, and in the meantime we have appointed Sieur Barre, Pere l'Escaye, a Jesuit residing in Poitiers, Pere Gaut of the Oratory, residing at Tours, to conduct the exorcisms, should such be necessary, and have given them an order to this effect.

"It is forbidden to all others to meddle with the said exorcisms, on pain of being punished according to law."

It will be seen from the above that His Grace the Archbishop of Bordeaux, in his enlightened and generous exercise of justice, had foreseen and provided for every possible contingency; so that as soon as his orders were made known to the exorcists the possession ceased at once and completely, and was no longer even talked of. Barre withdrew to Chinon, the senior canons rejoined their chapters, and the nuns, happily rescued for the time, resumed their life of retirement and tranquillity. The archbishop nevertheless urged on Grandier the prudence of effecting an exchange of benefices, but he replied that he would not at that moment change his simple living of Loudun for a bishopric.

Chapter VIII

The exposure of the plot was most prejudicial to the prosperity of the Ursuline community: spurious possession, far from bringing to their convent an increase of subscriptions and enhancing their reputation, as Mignon had promised, had ended for them in open shame, while in private they suffered from straitened circumstances, for the parents of their boarders hastened to withdraw their daughters from the convent, and the nuns in losing their pupils lost their sole source of income. Their, fall in the estimation of the public filled them with despair, and it leaked out that they had had several altercations with their director, during which they reproached him for having, by making them commit such a great sin, overwhelmed them with infamy and reduced them to misery, instead of securing for them the great spiritual and temporal advantages he had promised them. Mignon, although devoured by hate, was obliged to remain quiet, but he was none the less as determined as ever to have revenge, and as he was one of those men who never give up while a gleam of hope remains, and whom no waiting can tire, he bided his time, avoiding notice, apparently resigned to circumstances, but keeping his eyes fixed on Grandier, ready to seize on the first chance of recovering possession of the prey that had escaped his hands. And unluckily the chance soon presented itself.

It was now 1633: Richelieu was at the height of his power, carrying out his work of destruction, making castles fall before him where he could not make heads fall, in the spirit of John Knox's words, "Destroy the nests and the crows will disappear." Now one of these nests was the crenellated castle of Loudun, and Richelieu had therefore ordered its demolition.

The person appointed to carry out this order was a man such as those whom Louis XI. had employed fifty years earlier to destroy the feudal system, and Robespierre one hundred and fifty years later to destroy the aristocracy. Every woodman needs an axe, every reaper a sickle, and Richelieu found the instrument he required in de Laubardemont, Councillor of State.

But he was an instrument full of intelligence, detecting by the manner in which he was wielded the moving passion of the wielder, and adapting his whole nature with marvellous dexterity to gratify that passion according to the character of him whom it possessed; now by a rough and ready impetuosity, now by a deliberate and hidden advance; equally willing to strike with the sword or to poison by calumny, as the man who moved him lusted for the blood or sought to accomplish the dishonour of his victim.

M. de Laubardemont arrived at Loudun during the month of August 1633, and in order to carry out his mission addressed himself to Sieur Memin de Silly, prefect of the town, that old friend of the cardinal's whom Mignon and Barre, as we have said, had impressed so favourably. Memin saw in the arrival of Laubardemont a special intimation that it was the will of Heaven that the seemingly lost cause of those in whom he took such a warm interest should ultimately triumph. He presented Mignon and all his friends to M. Laubardemont, who received them with much cordiality. They talked of the mother superior, who was a relation, as we have seen, of M. de Laubardemont, and exaggerated the insult offered her by the decree of the archbishop, saying it was an affront to the whole family; and before long the one thing alone which occupied the thoughts of the conspirators and the councillor was how best to draw down upon Grandier the anger of the cardinal-duke. A way soon opened.

The Queen mother, Marie de Medici, had among her attendants a woman called Hammon, to whom, having once had occasion to speak, she had taken a fancy, and given a post near her person. In consequence of this whim, Hammon came to be regarded as a person of some importance in the queen's household. Hammon was a native of Loudun, and had passed the greater part of her youth there with her own people, who belonged to the lower classes. Grandier had been her confessor, and she attended his church, and as she was lively and clever he enjoyed talking to her, so that at length an intimacy sprang up between them. It so happened at a time when he and the other ministers were in momentary disgrace, that a satire full of biting wit and raillery appeared, directed especially against the cardinal, and this satire had been attributed to Hammon, who was known to share, as was natural, her mistress's hatred of Richelieu. Protected as she was by the queen's favour, the cardinal had found it impossible to punish Hammon, but he still cherished a deep resentment against her.

It now occurred to the conspirators to accuse Grandier of being the real author of the satire; and it was asserted that he had learned from Hammon all the details of the cardinal's private life, the knowledge of which gave so much point to the attack on him; if they could once succeed in making Richelieu believe this, Grandier was lost.

This plan being decided on, M. de Laubardemont was asked to visit the convent, and the devils knowing what an important personage he was, flocked thither to give him a worthy welcome. Accordingly, the nuns had attacks of the most indescribably violent convulsions, and M. de Laubardemont returned to Paris convinced as to the reality of their possession.

The first word the councillor of state said to the cardinal about Urbain Grandier showed him that he had taken useless trouble in inventing the story about the satire, for by the bare mention of his name he was able to arouse the cardinal's anger to any height he wished. The fact was, that when Richelieu had been Prior of Coussay he and Grandier had had a quarrel on a question of etiquette, the latter as priest of Loudun having claimed precedence over the prior, and carried his point. The cardinal had noted the affront in his bloodstained tablets, and at the first hint de Laubardemont found him as eager to bring about Grandier's ruin as was the councillor himself.

De Laubardemont was at once granted the following commission :

"Sieur de Laubardemont, Councillor of State and Privy Councillor, will betake himself to Loudun, and to whatever other places may be necessary, to institute proceedings against Grandier on all the charges formerly preferred against him, and on other facts which have since come to light, touching the possession by evil spirits of the Ursuline nuns of Loudun, and of other persons, who are said likewise to be tormented of devils through the evil practices of the said Grandier; he will diligently investigate everything from the beginning that has any bearing either on the said possession or on the exorcisms, and will forward to us his report thereon, and the reports and other documents sent in by former commissioners and delegates, and will be present at all future exorcisms, and take proper steps to obtain evidence of the said facts, that they may be clearly established; and, above all, will direct, institute, and carry through the said proceedings against Grandier and all others who have been involved with him in the said case, until definitive sentence be passed; and in spite of any appeal or countercharge this cause will not be delayed (but without prejudice to the right of appeal in other causes), on account of the nature of the crimes, and no regard will be paid to any request for postponement made by the said Grandier. His majesty commands all governors, provincial lieutenant-generals, bailiffs, seneschals, and other municipal authorities, and all subjects whom it may concern, to give every assistance in arresting and imprisoning all persons whom it may be necessary to put under constraint, if they shall be required so to do."

Furnished with this order, which was equivalent to a condemnation, de Laubardemont arrived at Laudun, the 5th of December, 1633, at nine o'clock in the evening; and to avoid being seen he alighted in a suburb at the house of one maitre Paul Aubin, king's usher, and son-in-law of Memin de Silly. His arrival was kept so secret that neither Grandier nor his friends knew of it, but Memin, Herve Menuau, and Mignon were notified, and immediately called on him. De Laubardemont received them, commission in hand, but broad as it was, it did not seem to them sufficient, for it contained no order for Grandier's arrest, and Grandier might fly. De Laubardemont, smiling at the idea that he could be so much in fault, drew from his pocket an order in duplicate, in case one copy should be lost, dated like the commission, November 30th, signed LOUIS, and countersigned PHILIPPEAUX. It was conceived in the following terms:

LOUIS, etc. etc.

"We have entrusted these presents to Sieur de Laubardemont, Privy Councillor, to empower the said Sieur de Laubardemont to arrest Grandier and his accomplices and imprison them in a secure place, with orders to all provosts, marshals, and other officers, and to all our subjects in general, to lend whatever assistance is necessary to carry out above order; and they are commanded by these presents to obey all orders given by the said Sieur; and all governors and lieutenants-general are also hereby commanded to furnish the said Sieur with whatever aid he may require at their hands."

This document being the completion of the other, it was immediately resolved, in order to show that they had the royal authority at their back, and as a preventive measure, to arrest Grandier at once, without any preliminary investigation. They hoped by this step to intimidate any official who might still be inclined to take Grandier's part, and any witness who might be disposed to testify in his favour. Accordingly, they immediately sent for Guillaume Aubin, Sieur de Lagrange and provost's lieutenant. De Laubardemont communicated to him the commission of the cardinal and the order of the king, and requested him to arrest Grandier early next morning. M. de Lagrange could not deny the two signatures, and answered that he would obey; but as he foresaw from their manner of going to work that the proceedings about to be instituted would be an assassination and not a fair trial, he sent, in spite of being a distant connection of Memin, whose daughter was married to his (Lagrange's) brother, to warn Grandier of the orders he had received. But Grandier with his usual intrepidity, while thanking Lagrange for his generous message, sent back word that, secure in his innocence and relying on the justice of God, he was determined to stand his ground.

So Grandier remained, and his brother, who slept beside him, declared that his sleep that night was as quiet as usual. The next morning he rose, as was his habit, at six o'clock, took his breviary in his hand, and went out with the intention of attending matins at the church of Sainte-Croix. He had hardly put his foot over the threshold before Lagrange, in the presence of Memin, Mignon, and the other conspirators, who had come out to gloat over the sight, arrested him in the name of the king. He was at once placed in the custody of Jean Pouguet, an archer in His Majesty's guards, and of the archers of the provosts of Loudun and Chinon, to be taken to the castle at Angers. Meanwhile a search was instituted, and the royal seal affixed to the doors of his apartments, to his presses, his other articles of furniture- in fact, to every thing and place in the house; but nothing was found that tended to compromise him, except an essay against the celibacy of priests, and two sheets of paper whereon were written in another hand than his, some love-poems in the taste of that time.

Urbain Grandier

Chapter IX

For four months Grandier languished in prison, and, according to the report of Michelon, commandant of Angers, and of Pierre Bacher, his confessor, he was, during the whole period, a model of patience and firmness, passing his days in reading good books or in writing prayers and meditations, which were afterwards produced at his trial. Meanwhile, in spite of the urgent appeals of Jeanne Esteye, mother of the accused, who, although seventy years of age, seemed to recover her youthful strength and activity in the desire to save her son, Laubardemont continued the examination, which was finished on April 4th. Urbain was then brought back from Angers to Loudun.

An extraordinary cell had been prepared for him in a house belonging to Mignon, and which had formerly been occupied by a sergeant named Bontems, once clerk to Trinquant, who had been a witness for the prosecution in the first trial. It was on the topmost story; the windows had been walled up, leaving only one small slit open, and even this opening was secured by enormous iron bars; and by an exaggeration of caution the mouth of the fireplace was furnished with a grating, lest the devils should arrive through the chimney to free the sorcerer from his chains. Furthermore, two holes in the corners of the room, so formed that they were unnoticeable from within, allowed a constant watch to be kept over Grandier's movements by Bontem's wife, a precaution by which they hoped to learn something that would help them in the coming exorcisms. In this room, lying on a little straw, and almost without light, Grandier wrote the following letter to his mother:

> "My Mother,—I received your letter and everything you sent me except the woollen stockings. I endure any affliction with patience, and feel more pity for you than for myself. I am very much inconvenienced for want of a bed; try and have mine brought to me, for my mind will give way if my body has no rest: if you can, send me a breviary, a Bible, and a St. Thomas for my consolation; and above all, do not grieve for me. I trust that, God will bring my innocence to light.

Urbain Grandier

Commend me to my brother and sister, and all our good friends.—I am, mother, your dutiful son and servant,

"Grandier"

While Grandier had been in prison at Angers the cases of possession at the convent had miraculously multiplied, for it was no longer only the superior and Sister Claire who had fallen a prey to the evil spirits, but also several other sisters, who were divided into three groups as follows, and separated:—

The superior, with Sisters Louise des Anges and Anne de Sainte-Agnes, were sent to the house of Sieur Delaville, advocate, legal adviser to the sisterhood; Sisters Claire and Catherine de la Presentation were placed in the house of Canon Maurat; Sisters Elisabeth de la Croix, Monique de Sainte-Marthe, Jeanne du Sainte-Esprit, and Seraphique Archer were in a third house.

A general supervision was undertaken by Memin's sister, the wife of Moussant, who was thus closely connected with two of the greatest enemies of the accused, and to her Bontems' wife told all that the superior needed to know about Grandier. Such was the manner of the sequestration!

The choice of physicians was no less extraordinary. Instead of calling in the most skilled practitioners of Angers, Tours, Poitiers, or Saumur, all of them, except Daniel Roger of Loudun, came from the surrounding villages, and were men of no education: one of them, indeed, had failed to obtain either degree or licence, and had been obliged to leave Saumur in consequence; another had been employed in a small shop to take goods home, a position he had exchanged for the more lucrative one of quack.

There was just as little sense of fairness and propriety shown in the choice of the apothecary and surgeon. The apothecary, whose name was Adam, was Mignon's first cousin, and had been one of the witnesses for the prosecution at Grandier's first trial; and as on that occasion—he had libelled a young girl of Loudun, he had been sentenced by a decree of Parliament to make a public apology. And yet, though his hatred of Grandier in consequence of this humiliation was so well known,—perhaps for that very reason, it was to him the duty of dispensing and administering the prescriptions was entrusted, no one supervising the work even so far as to see that the proper doses were given, or taking note whether for sedatives he did not sometimes substitute stimulating and exciting drugs, capable of producing real convulsions. The surgeon Mannouri was still more unsuitable, for he was a nephew of Memin de Silly, and brother of the nun who had offered the most determined opposition to Grandier's demand for sequestration of the possessed sisters, during the second series of exorcisms. In vain did the mother and brother of the accused present petitions setting forth the incapacity of the doctors and the hatred of Grandier professed by the apothecary; they could not, even at their own expense, obtain certified copies of any of these petitions, although they had witnesses ready to prove that Adam had once in his ignorance dispensed crocus metallorum for crocus mantis—a mistake which had caused the death of the patient for whom the prescription was made up. In short, so determined were the conspirators that this time Grandier should be done to death, that they had not even the decency to conceal the infamous methods by which they had arranged to attain this result.

The examination was carried on with vigour. As one of the first formalities would be the identification of the accused, Grandier published a memorial in which he recalled the case of Saint-Anastasius at the Council of Tyre, who had been accused of immorality by a fallen woman whom he had never seen before. When this woman entered the hall of justice in order to swear to her deposition, a priest named Timothy went up to her and began to talk to her as if he were Anastasius; falling into the trap, she answered as if she recognised him, and thus the innocence of the saint was shown forth. Grandier therefore demanded that two or three persons of his own height and complexion should be dressed exactly like himself, and with him should be allowed to confront the nuns. As he had never seen any of them, and was almost certain they had never seen him, they would not be able, he felt sure, to point him out with certainty, in spite of the allegations of undue intimacy with themselves they brought against him. This demand showed such conscious innocence that it was embarrassing to answer, so no notice was taken of it.

Meanwhile the Bishop of Poitiers, who felt much elated at getting the better of the Archbishop of Bordeaux, who of course was powerless against an order issued by the cardinal-duke, took exception to Pere l'Escaye and Pere Gaut, the exorcists appointed by his superior, and named instead his own chaplain, who had been judge at Grandier's first trial, and had passed sentence on him, and Pere Lactance, a Franciscan monk. These two, making no secret of the side with which they sympathised, put up on their arrival at Nicolas Moussant's, one of Grandier's most bitter enemies; on the following day they went to the superior's apartments and began their exorcisms. The first time the superior opened her lips to reply, Pere Lactance perceived that she knew almost no Latin, and consequently would not shine during the exorcism, so he ordered her to answer in French, although he still continued to exorcise her in Latin; and when someone was bold enough to object, saying that the devil, according to the ritual, knew all languages living and dead, and ought to reply in the same language in which he was addressed, the father declared that the incongruity was caused by the pact, and that moreover some devils were more ignorant than peasants.

Following these exorcists, and two Carmelite monks, named Pierre de Saint-Thomas and Pierre de Saint-Mathurin, who had, from the very beginning, pushed their way in when anything was going on, came four Capuchins sent by Pere Joseph, head of the Franciscans, "His grey Eminence," as he was called, and whose names were Peres Luc, Tranquille, Potais, and Elisee; so that a much more rapid advance could be made than hitherto by carrying on the exorcisms in four different places at once—viz., in the convent, and in the churches of Sainte-Croix, Saint-Pierre du Martroy, and Notre-Dame du Chateau. Very little of importance took place, however, on the first two occasions, the 15th and 16th of April; for the declarations of the doctors were most vague and indefinite, merely saying that the things they had seen were supernatural, surpassing their knowledge and the rules of medicine.

Urbain Grandier

The ceremony of the 23rd April presented, however, some points of interest. The superior, in reply to the interrogations of Pere Lactance, stated that the demon had entered her body under the forms of a cat, a dog, a stag, and a buck-goat.

"Quoties?" (How often?), inquired the exorcist.

"I didn't notice the day," replied the superior, mistaking the word quoties for quando (when).

It was probably to revenge herself for this error that the superior declared the same day that Grandier had on his body five marks made by the devil, and that though his body was else insensible to pain, he was vulnerable at those spots. Mannouri, the surgeon, was therefore ordered to verify this assertion, and the day appointed for the verification was the 26th.

In virtue of this mandate Mannouri presented himself early on that day at Grandier's prison, caused him to be stripped naked and cleanly shaven, then ordered him to be laid on a table and his eyes bandaged. But the devil was wrong again: Grandier had only two marks, instead of five—one on the shoulder-blade, and the other on the thigh.

Then took place one of the most abominable performances that can be imagined. Mannouri held in his hand a probe, with a hollow handle, into which the needle slipped when a spring was touched: when Mannouri applied the probe to those parts of Grandier's body which, according to the superior, were insensible, he touched the spring, and the needle, while seeming to bury itself in the flesh, really retreated into the handle, thus causing no pain; but when he touched one of the marks said to be vulnerable, he left the needle fixed, and drove it in to the depth of several inches. The first time he did this it drew from poor Grandier, who was taken unprepared, such a piercing cry that it was heard in the street by the crowd which had gathered round the door. From the mark on the shoulder-blade with which he had commenced, Mannouri passed to that on the thigh, but though he plunged the needle in to its full depth Grandier

Urbain Grandier

uttered neither cry nor groan, but went on quietly repeating a prayer, and notwithstanding that Mannouri stabbed him twice more through each of the two marks, he could draw nothing from his victim but prayers for his tormentors.

M. de Laubardemont was present at this scene.

The next day the devil was addressed in such forcible terms that an acknowledgment was wrung from him that Grandier's body bore, not five, but two marks only; and also, to the vast admiration of the spectators, he was able this time to indicate their precise situation.

Unfortunately for the demon, a joke in which he indulged on this occasion detracted from the effect of the above proof of cleverness. Having been asked why he had refused to speak on the preceding Saturday, he said he had not been at Loudun on that day, as the whole morning he had been occupied in accompanying the soul of a certain Le Proust, attorney to the Parliament of Paris, to hell. This answer awoke such doubts in the breasts of some of the laymen present that they took the trouble to examine the register of deaths, and found that no one of the name of Le Proust, belonging to any profession whatever, had died on that date. This discovery rendered the devil less terrible, and perhaps less amusing.

Meantime the progress of the other exorcisms met with like interruptions. Pere Pierre de Saint Thomas, who conducted the operations in the Carmelite church, asked one of the possessed sisters where Grandier's books of magic were; she replied that they were kept at the house of a certain young girl, whose name she gave, and who was the same to whom Adam had been forced to apologise. De Laubardemont, Moussant, Herve, and Meunau hastened at once to the house indicated, searched the rooms and the presses, opened the chests and the wardrobes and all the secret places in the house, but in vain. On their return to the church, they reproached the devil for having deceived them, but he explained that a niece of the young woman had removed the books. Upon this, they hurried to the niece's dwelling, but unluckily she was not at home, having spent the whole day at a certain church making her devotions, and when they went thither, the priests and attendants averred that she had not gone out all day; so notwithstanding the desire of the exorcists to oblige Adam they were forced to let the matter drop.

These two false statements increased the number of unbelievers; but it was announced that a most interesting performance would take place on May 4th; indeed, the programme when issued was varied enough to arouse general curiosity. Asmodeus was to raise the superior two feet from the ground, and the fiends Eazas and Cerberus, in emulation of their leader, would do as much for two other nuns; while a fourth devil, named Beherit, would go farther still, and, greatly daring, would attack M. de Laubardemont himself, and, having spirited his councillor's cap from his head, would hold it suspended in the air for the space of a Misereye. Furthermore, the exorcists announced that six of the strongest men in the town would try to prevent the contortions of the, weakest of the convulsed nuns, and would fail.

It need hardly be said that the prospect of such an entertainment filled the church on the appointed day to overflowing. Pere Lactance began by calling on Asmodeus to fulfil his promise of raising the superior from the ground. She began, hereupon, to perform various evolutions on her mattress, and at one moment it seemed as if she were really suspended in the air; but one of the spectators lifted her dress and showed that she was only standing on tiptoe, which, though it might be clever, was not miraculous. Shouts of laughter rent the air, which had such an intimidating effect on Eazas and Cerberus that not all the adjurations of the exorcists could extract the slightest response. Beherit was their last hope, and he replied that he was prepared to lift up M. de Laubardemont's cap, and would do so before the expiration of a quarter of an hour.

We must here remark that this time the exorcisms took place in the evening, instead of in the morning as hitherto; and it was now growing dark, and darkness is favourable to illusions. Several of the unbelieving ones present, therefore, began to call attention to the fact that the quarter of an hour's delay would necessitate the employment of artificial light during the next scene. They also noticed that M. de Laubardemont had seated himself apart and immediately beneath one of the arches in the vaulted roof, through which a hole had been drilled for the passage of the bell-rope. They therefore slipped out of the church, and up into the belfry, where they hid. In a few moments a man appeared who began to work at something. They sprang on him and seized his wrists, and found in one of his hands a thin line of horsehair, to one end of which a hook was attached. The holder being frightened, dropped the line and fled, and although M. de Laubardemont, the exorcists, and the spectators waited, expecting every moment that the cap would rise into the air, it remained quite firm on the owner's head, to the no small confusion of Pere Lactance, who, all unwitting of the fiasco, continued to adjure Beherit to keep his word—of course without the least effect.

Altogether, this performance of May 4th, went anything but smoothly. Till now no trick had succeeded; never before had the demons been such bunglers. But the exorcists were sure that the last trick would go off without a hitch. This was, that a nun, held by six men chosen for their strength, would succeed in extricating herself from their grasp, despite their utmost efforts. Two Carmelites and two Capuchins went through the audience and selected six giants from among the porters and messengers of the town.

This time the devil answered expectations by showing that if he was not clever he was strong, for although the six men tried to hold her down upon her mattress, the superior was seized with such terrible convulsions that she escaped from their hands, throwing down one of those who tried to detain her. This experiment, thrice renewed, succeeded thrice, and belief seemed about to return to the assembly, when a physician of Saumur named Duncan, suspecting trickery, entered the choir, and, ordering the six men to retire, said he was going to try and hold the superior down unaided, and if she escaped from his hands he would make a public apology for his unbelief. M. de Laubardemont tried to prevent this test, by objecting to Duncan as an atheist, but as Duncan was greatly respected on account of his skill and probity, there was such an outcry at this interference from the entire audience that the commissioner was forced to let him have his way. The six porters were therefore dismissed, but instead of resuming their places among the spectators they left the church by the sacristy, while Duncan approaching the bed on which the superior had again lain down, seized her by the wrist, and making certain that he had a firm hold, he told the exorcists to begin.

Never up to that time had it been so clearly shown that the conflict going on was between public opinion and the private aims of a few. A hush fell on the church; everyone stood motionless in silent expectancy.

The moment Pere Lactance uttered the sacred words the convulsions of the superior recommenced; but it seemed as if Duncan had more strength than his six predecessors together, for twist and writhe and struggle as she would, the superior's wrist remained none the less firmly clasped in Duncan's hand. At length she fell back on her bed exhausted, exclaiming!"

"It's no use, it's no use! He's holding me!"

Release her arm! "shouted Pere Lactance in a rage. "How can the convulsions take place if you hold her that way?"

"If she is really possessed by a demon," answered Duncan aloud, "he should be stronger than I; for it is stated in the ritual that among the symptoms of possession is strength beyond one's years, beyond one's condition, and beyond what is natural."

"That is badly argued," said Lactance sharply: "a demon outside the body is indeed stronger than you, but when enclosed in a weak frame such as this it cannot show such strength, for its efforts are proportioned to the strength of the body it possesses."

"Enough!" said M. de Laubardemont ; "we did not come here to argue with philosophers, but to build up the faith of Christians."

With that he rose up from his chair amidst a terrible uproar, and the assembly dispersed in the utmost disorder, as if they were leaving a theatre rather than a church.

The ill success of this exhibition caused a cessation of events of interest for some days. The result was that a great number of noblemen and other people of quality who had come to Loudun expecting to see wonders and had been shown only commonplace transparent tricks, began to think it was not worth while remaining any longer, and went their several ways—a defection much bewailed by Pere Tranquille in a little work which he published on this affair.

> "Many," he says, "came to see miracles at Loudun, but finding the devils did not give them the signs they expected, they went away dissatisfied, and swelled the numbers of the unbelieving."

It was determined, therefore, in order to keep the town full, to predict some great event which would revive curiosity and increase faith. Pere Lactance therefore announced that on the 20th of May three of the seven devils dwelling in the superior would come out, leaving three wounds in her left side, with corresponding holes in her chemise, bodice, and dress. The three parting devils were Asmodeus, Gresil des Trones, and Aman des Puissances. He added that the superior's hands would be bound behind her back at the time the wounds were given.

On the appointed day the church of Sainte-Croix was filled to overflowing with sightseers curious to know if the devils would keep their promises better this time than the last. Physicians were invited to examine the superior's side and her clothes; and amongst those who came forward was Duncan, whose presence guaranteed the public against deception; but none of the exorcists ventured to exclude him, despite the hatred in which they held him—a hatred which they would have made him feel if he had not been under the special protection of Marshal Breze. The physicians having completed their examination, gave the following certificate:—

"We have found no wound in the patient's side, no rent in her vestments, and our search revealed no sharp instrument hidden in the folds of her dress."

These preliminaries having been got through, Pere Lactance questioned her in French for nearly two hours, her answers being in the same language. Then he passed from questions to adjurations: on this, Duncan came forward, and said a promise had been given that the superior's hands should be tied behind her back, in order that there might be no room for suspicion of fraud, and that the moment had now arrived to keep that promise. Pere Lactance admitted the justice of the demand, but said as there were many present who had never seen the superior in convulsions such as afflicted the possessed, it would be only fair that she should be exorcised for their satisfaction before binding her. Accordingly he began to repeat the form of exorcism, and the superior was immediately attacked by frightful convulsions, which in a few minutes produced complete exhaustion, so that she fell on her face to the ground, and turning on her left arm and side, remained motionless some instants, after which she uttered a low cry, followed by a groan. The physicians approached her, and Duncan seeing her take away her hand from her left side, seized her arm, and found that the tips of her fingers were stained with blood. They then examined her clothing and body, and found her dress, bodice, and chemise cut through in three places, the cuts being less than an inch long. There were also three scratches beneath the left breast, so slight as to be scarcely more than skin deep, the middle one being a barleycorn in length; still, from all three a sufficient quantity of blood had oozed to stain the chemise above them.

This time the fraud was so glaring that even de Laubardemont exhibited some signs of confusion because of the number and quality of the spectators. He would not, however, allow the doctors to include in their report their opinion as to the manner in which the wounds were inflicted; but Grandier protested against this in a Statement of Facts, which he drew up during the night, and which was distributed next day.

Urbain Grandier

It was as follows :

"That if the superior had not groaned the physicians would not have removed her clothes, and would have suffered her to be bound, without having the least idea that the wounds were already made; that then the exorcists would have commanded the devils to come forth, leaving the traces they had promised; that the superior would then have gone through the most extraordinary contortions of which she was capable, and have had a long fit of, convulsions, at the end of which she would have been delivered from the three demons, and the wounds would have been found in her body; that her groans, which had betrayed her, had by God's will thwarted the best-laid plans of men and devils. Why do you suppose," he went on to ask, "that clean incised wounds, such as a sharp blade would make, 'were chosen for a token, seeing that the wounds left by devils resemble burns? Was it not because it was easier for the superior to conceal a lancet with which to wound herself slightly, than to conceal any instrument sufficiently heated to burn her? Why do you think the left side was chosen rather than the forehead and nose, if not because she could not give herself a wound in either of those places without being seen by all the spectators? Why was the left side rather than the right chosen, if it were not that it was easier for the superior to wound herself with her right hand, which she habitually used, in the left side than in the right? Why did she turn on her left side and arm and remain so long in that position, if it were not to hide from the bystanders the instrument with which she wounded herself? What do you think caused her to groan, in spite of all her resolution, if it were not the pain of the wound she gave herself? for the most courageous cannot repress a shudder when the surgeon opens a vein. Why were her finger-tips stained with blood, if it were not that the secreted blade was so small that the fingers which held it could not escape being reddened by the blood it caused to flow? How came it that the wounds were so superficial that they barely went deeper than the cuticle, while devils are known to rend and tear demoniacs when leaving them, if it were not that the superior did not hate herself enough to inflict deep and dangerous wounds?"

Despite this logical protest from Grandier and the barefaced knavery of the exorcist, M. de Laubardemont prepared a report of the expulsion of the three devils, Asmodeus, Gresil, and Aman, from the body of sister Jeanne des Anges, through three wounds below the region of the heart; a report which was afterwards shamelessly used against Grandier, and of which the memorandum still exists, a monument, not so much of credulity and superstition, as of hatred and revenge. Pere Lactance, in order to allay the suspicions which the pretended miracle had aroused among the eye-wittnesses, asked Balaam, one of the four demons who still remained in the superior's body, the following day, why Asmodeus and his two companions had gone out against their promise, while the superior's face and hands were hidden from the people.

"To lengthen the incredulity of certain people," answered Balaam.

As for Pere Tranquille, he published a little volume describing the whole affair, in which, with the irresponsible frivolity of a true Capuchin, he poked fun at those who could not swallow the miracles wholesale.

"They had every reason to feel vexed," he said, "at the small courtesy or civility shown by the demons to persons of their merit and station; but if they had examined their consciences, perhaps they would have found the real reason of their discontent, and, turning their anger against themselves, would have done penance for having come to the exorcisms led by a depraved moral sense and a prying spirit."

Nothing remarkable happened from the 20th May till the 13th June, a day which became noteworthy by reason of the superior's vomiting a quill a finger long. It was doubtless this last miracle which brought the Bishop of Poitiers to Loudun, "not," as he said to those who came to pay their respects to him, "to examine into the genuineness of the possession, but to force those to believe who still doubted, and to discover the classes which Urbain had founded to teach the black art to pupils of both sexes."

Thereupon the opinion began to prevail among the people that it would be prudent to believe in the possession, since the king, the cardinal-duke, and the bishop believed in it, and that continued doubt would lay them open to the charges of disloyalty to their king and their Church, and of complicity in the crimes of Grandier, and thus draw down upon them the ruthless punishment of Laubardemont.

"The reason we feel so certain that our work is pleasing to God is that it is also pleasing to the king," wrote Pere Lactance.

The arrival of the bishop was followed by a new exorcism; and of this an eye-witness, who was a good Catholic and a firm believer in possession, has left us a written description, more interesting than any we could give. We shall present it to our readers, word for word, as it stands:—

> "On Friday, 23rd June 1634, on the Eve of Saint John, about 3 p.m., the Lord Bishop of Poitiers and M. de Laubardemont being present in the church of Sainte-Croix of Loudun, to continue the exorcisms of the Ursuline nuns, by order of M, de Laubardemont, commissioner, Urbain Grandier, priest-in-charge, accused and denounced as a magician by the said possessed nuns, was brought from his prison to the said church.

> "There were produced by the said commissioner to the said Urbain Grandier four pacts mentioned several times by the said possessed nuns at the preceding exorcisms, which the devils who possessed the nuns declared they had made with the said Grandier on several occasions: there was one in especial which Leviathan gave up on Saturday the 17th inst., composed of an infant's heart procured at a witches' sabbath, held in Orleans in 1631; the ashes of a consecrated

wafer, blood, etc., of the said Grandier, whereby Leviathan asserted he had entered the body of the sister, Jeanne des Anges, the superior of the said nuns, and took possession of her with his coadjutors Beherit, Eazas, and Balaam, on December 8th, 1632. Another such pact was composed of the pips of Grenada oranges, and was given up by Asmodeus and a number of other devils. It had been made to hinder Beherit from keeping his promise to lift the commissioner's hat two inches from his head and to hold it there the length of a Miseyere, as a sign that he had come out of the nun. On all these pacts being shown to the said Grandier, he said, without astonishment, but with much firmness and resolution, that he had no knowledge of them whatever, that he had never made them, and had not the skill by which to make them, that he had held no communication with devils, and knew nothing of what they were talking about. A report of all this being made and shown to him, he signed it.

"This done, they brought all the possessed nuns, to the number of eleven or twelve, including three lay sisters, also possessed, into the choir of the said church, accompanied by a great many monks, Carmelites, Capuchins, and Franciscans; and by three physicians and a surgeon. The sisters on entering made some wanton remarks, calling Grandier their master, and exhibiting great delight at seeing him.

"Thereupon Pere Lactance and Gabriel, a Franciscan brother, and one of the exorcists, exhorted all present with great fervour to lift up their hearts to God and to make an act of contrition for the offences committed against His divine majesty, and to pray that the number of their sins might not be an obstacle to the fulfilment of the plans which He in His providence had formed for the promotion of His glory on that occasion, and to give outward proof of their heartfelt grief by repeating the Confiteor as a preparation for the blessing of the Lord Bishop of Poitiers. This having been done, he went on to say that the matter in question was of such moment and so important in its relation to the great truths of the Roman Catholic Church, that this consideration alone ought to be sufficient to excite their devotion; and furthermore, that the affliction of these poor sisters was so peculiar and had lasted so long, that charity impelled all those who had the right to work for their deliverance and the expulsion of the devils, to employ the power entrusted to them with their office in accomplishing so worthy a task by the forms of exorcism prescribed by the Church to its ministers; then addressing Grandier, he said that he having been anointed as a priest belonged to this number, and that he ought to help with all his power and with all his energy, if the bishop were pleased to allow him to do so, and to remit his suspension from authority. The bishop having granted permission, the Franciscan friar offered a stole to Grandier, who, turning towards the prelate, asked him if he might take it. On receiving a reply in the affirmative, he passed it round his neck, and on being offered a copy of the ritual, he asked permission to accept it as before, and received the bishop's blessing, prostrating himself at his feet to kiss them; whereupon the Veni Creator Spiritus having been sung, he rose, and addressing the bishop, asked—

"'My lord, whom am I to exorcise?'"

The said bishop having replied—

"'These maidens.'

" Grandier again asked—

"'What maidens?'

"'The possessed maidens,' was the answer.

"'That is to say, my lord,' said he; "that I am obliged to believe in the fact of possession. The Church believes in it, therefore I too believe;

but I cannot believe that a sorcerer can cause a Christian to be possessed unless the Christian consent.'

"Upon this, some of those present exclaimed that it was heretical to profess such a belief; that the contrary was indubitable, believed by the whole Church and approved by the Sorbonne. To which he replied that his mind on that point was not yet irrevocably made up, that what he had said was simply his own idea, and that in any case he submitted to the opinion of the whole body of which he was only a member; that nobody was declared a heretic for having doubts, but only for persisting in them, and that what he had advanced was only for the purpose of drawing an assurance from the bishop that in doing what he was about to do he would not be abusing the authority of the Church. Sister Catherine having been brought to him by the Franciscan as the most ignorant of all the nuns, and the least open to the suspicion of being acquainted with Latin, he began the exorcism in the form prescribed by the ritual. But as soon as he began to question her he was interrupted, for all the other nuns were attacked by devils, and uttered strange and terrible noises. Amongst the rest, Sister Claire came near, and reproached him for his blindness and obstinacy, so that he was forced to leave the nun with whom he had begun, and address his words to the said Sister Claire, who during the entire duration of the exorcism continued to talk at random, without paying any heed to Grandier's words, which were also interrupted by the mother superior, to whom he of last gave attention, leaving Sister Claire. But it is to be noted that before beginning to exorcise the superior, he said, speaking in Latin as heretofore, that knowing she understood Latin, he would question her in Greek. To which the devil replied by the mouth of the possessed

"'Ah! how clever you are! You know it was one of the first conditions of our pact that I was not to answer in Greek.'

"Upon this, he cried, 'O pulchra illusio, egregica evasio!' (O superb fraud, outrageous evasion!)

"He was then told that he was permitted to exorcise in Greek, provided he first wrote down what he wished to say, and the superior hereupon said that he should be answered in what language he pleased; but it was impossible, for as soon as he opened his mouth all the nuns recommenced their shrieks and paroxysms, showing unexampled despair, and giving way to convulsions, which in each patient assumed a new form, and persisting in accusing Grandier of using magic and the black art to torment them; offering to wring his neck if they were allowed, and trying to outrage his feelings in every possible way. But this being against the prohibitions of the Church, the priests and monks present worked with the utmost zeal to calm the frenzy which had seized on the nuns. Grandier meanwhile remained calm and unmoved, gazing fixedly at the maniacs, protesting his innocence, and praying to God for protection. Then addressing himself to the bishop and M. de Laubardemont, he implored them by the ecclesiastical and royal authority of which they were the ministers to command these demons to wring his neck, or at least to put a mark in his forehead, if he were guilty of the crime of which they accused him, that the glory of God might be shown forth, the authority of the Church vindicated, and himself brought to confusion, provided that the nuns did not touch him with their hands. But to this the bishop and the commissioner would not consent, because they did not want to be responsible for what might happen to him, neither would they expose the authority of the Church to the wiles of the devils, who might have made some pact on that point with Grandier. Then the exorcists, to the number of eight, having commanded the devils to be silent and to cease their tumult, ordered a brazier to be brought, and into this they threw the pacts one by one, whereupon the convulsions returned with such awful violence and confused cries, rising into frenzied shrieks, and accompanied by such horrible contortions, that the scene might have been taken for an orgy of witches, were it not for the sanctity of the place and the character of those present, of whom Grandier, in outward seeming at least, was the least amazed of any, although he had the most reason. The devils continued their accusations, citing the places, the days, and the hours of their intercourse with him; the first spell he cast on them, his scandalous behaviour, his insensibility, his abjurations of God and the faith. To all this he calmly returned that these accusations were calumnies, and all the more unjust considering his profession; that he renounced Satan and all his fiends, having neither knowledge nor comprehension of them; that in spite of all he was a Christian, and what was more, an anointed priest; that though he knew himself to be a sinful man, yet his trust was in God and in His Christ; that he had never indulged in such abominations, end that it would be impossible to furnish any pertinent and convincing proof of his guilt.

"At this point no words could express what the senses perceived; eyes and ears received an impression of being surrounded by furies such as had never been gathered together before; and unless accustomed to such ghastly scenes as those who sacrifice to demons, no one could keep his mind free from astonishment and horror in the midst of such a spectacle. Grandier alone remained unchanged through it all, seemingly insensible to the monstrous exhibitions, singing hymns to the Lord with the rest of the people, as confident as if he were guarded by legions of angels. One of the demons cried out that Beelzebub was standing between him and Pere Tranquille the Capuchin, upon which Grandier said to the demon—

"'Obmutescas!' (Hold thy peace).

"Upon this the demon began to curse, and said that was their watchword; but they could not hold their peace, because God was infinitely powerful, and the powers of hell could not prevail against Him. Thereupon they all struggled to get at Grandier, threatening to tear him limb from limb, to point out his marks, to strangle him although he was their master; whereupon he seized a chance to say he was neither their master nor their servant, and that it was incredible that they should in the same breath acknowledge him for their master and express a desire to strangle him: on hearing this, the frenzy of the nuns reached its height, and they kicked their slippers into his face.

"'Just look!' said he; 'the shoes drop from the hoofs of their own accord.'

"At length, had it not been for the help and interposition of people in the choir, the nuns in their frenzy would have taken the life of the chief personage in this spectacle; so there was no choice but to take him away from the church and the furies who threatened his life. He was therefore brought back to prison about six o'clock in the evening, and the rest of the day the exorcists were employed in calming the poor sisters—a task of no small difficulty."

Everyone did not regard the possessed sisters with the indulgent eye of the author of the above narrative, and many saw in this terrible exhibition of hysteria and convulsions an infamous and sacrilegious orgy, at which revenge ran riot. There was such difference of opinion about it that it was considered necessary to publish the following proclamation by means of placards on July 2nd:

> "All persons, of whatever rank or profession, are hereby expressly forbidden to traduce, or in any way malign, the nuns and other persons at Loudun possessed by evil spirits; or their exorcists; or those who accompany them either to the places appointed for exorcism or elsewhere; in any form or manner whatever, on pain of a fine of ten thousand livres, or a larger sum and corporal punishment should the case so require; and in order that no one may plead ignorance hereof, this proclamation will be read and published to-day from the pulpits of all the churches, and copies affixed to the church doors and in other suitable public places.
>
> " Done at Loudun, July 2nd, 1634."

This order had great influence with worldly folk, and from that moment, whether their belief was strengthened or not, they no longer dared to express any incredulity. But in spite of that, the judges were put to shame, for the nuns themselves began to repent; and on the day following the impious scene above described, just as Pere Lactanee began to exorcise Sister Claire in the castle chapel, she rose, and turning towards the congregation, while tears ran down her cheeks, said in a voice that could be heard by all present, that she was going to speak the truth at last in the sight of Heaven.

Thereupon she confessed that all that she had said during the last fortnight against Grandier was calumnious and false, and that all her actions had been done at the instigation of the Franciscan Pere Lactance, the director, Mignon, and the Carmelite brothers. Pere Lactance, not in the least taken aback, declared that her confession was a fresh wile of the devil to save her master Grandier. She then made an urgent appeal to the bishop and to M. de Laubardemont, asking to be sequestered and placed in charge of other priests than those who had destroyed her soul, by making her bear false witness against an innocent man; but they only laughed at the pranks the devil was playing, and ordered her to be at once taken back to the house in which she was then living. When she heard this order, she darted out of the choir, trying to escape through the church door, imploring those present to come to her assistance and save her from everlasting damnation. But such terrible fruit had the proclamation borne that noon dared respond, so she was recaptured and taken back to the house in which she was sequestered, never to leave it again.

Chapter X

The next day a still more extraordinary scene took place. While M. de Laubardemont was questioning one of the nuns, the superior came down into the court, barefooted; in her chemise, and a cord round her neck; and there she remained for two hours, in the midst of a fearful storm, not shrinking before lightning, thunder, or rain, but waiting till M. de Laubardemont and the other exorcists should come out. At length the door opened and the royal commissioner appeared, whereupon Sister Jeanne des Anges, throwing herself at his feet, declared she had not sufficient strength to play the horrible part they had made her learn any longer, and that before God and man she declared Urbain Grandier innocent, saying that all the hatred which she and her companions had felt against him arose from the baffled desires which his comeliness awoke—desires which the seclusion of conventional life made still more ardent. M. de Laubardemont threatened her with the full weight of his displeasure, but she answered, weeping bitterly, that all she now dreaded was her sin, for though the mercy of the Saviour was great, she felt that the crime she had committed could never be pardoned. M. de Laubardemont exclaimed that it was the demon who dwelt in her who was speaking, but she replied that the only demon by whom she had even been possessed was the spirit of vengeance, and that it was indulgence in her own evil thoughts, and not a pact with the devil, which had admitted him into her heart.

With these words she withdrew slowly, still weeping, and going into the garden, attached one end of the cord round her neck to the branch of a tree, and hanged herself. But some of the sisters who had followed her cut her down before life was extinct.

The same day an order for her strict seclusion was issued for her as for Sister Claire, and the circumstances that she was a relation of M. de Laubardemont did not avail to lessen her punishment in view of the gravity of her fault.

Urbain Grandier

It was impossible to continue the exorcisms other nuns might be tempted to follow the example, of the superior and Sister Claire, and in that case all would be lost. And besides, was not Urbain Grandier well and duly convicted? It was announced, therefore, that the examination had proceeded far enough, and that the judges would consider the evidence and deliver judgment.

This long succession of violent and irregular breaches of law procedure, the repeated denials of his claim to justice, the refusal to let his witnesses appear, or to listen to his defence, all combined to convince Grandier that his ruin was determined on; for the case had gone so far and had attained such publicity that it was necessary either to punish him as a sorcerer and magician or to render a royal commissioner, a bishop, an entire community of nuns, several monks of various orders, many judges of high reputation, and laymen of birth and standing, liable to the penalties incurred by calumniators. But although, as this conviction grew, he confronted it with resignation, his courage did not fail,—and holding it to be his duty as a man and a Christian to defend his life and honour to the end, he drew up and published another memorandum, headed Reasons for Acquittal, and had copies laid before his judges. It was a weighty and, impartial summing up of the whole case, such as a stranger might have written, and began, with these words.

"I entreat you in all humility to consider deliberately and with attention what the Psalmist says in Psalm 82, where he exhorts judges to fulfil their charge with absolute rectitude; they being themselves mere mortals who will one day have to appear before God, the sovereign judge of the universe, to give an account of their administration. The Lord's Anointed speaks to you to-day who are sitting in judgment, and says—

"'God standeth in the congregation of the mighty: He judgeth among the gods.

"'How long will ye judge unjustly, and accept the persons of the wicked?

"'Defend the poor and fatherless: do justice to the afflicted and needy.

"'Deliver the poor and needy: rid them out of the hand of the wicked.

"'I have said, Ye are gods; and all of you are children of the Most High.

"'But ye shall die like men, and fall like one of the princes.'"

But this appeal, although convincing and dignified, had no influence upon the commission; and on the 18th of August the following verdict and sentence was pronounced:—

"We have declared, and do hereby declare, Urbain Grandier duly accused and convicted of the crimes of magic and witchcraft, and of causing the persons of certain Ursuline nuns of this town and of other females to become possessed of evil spirits, wherefrom other crimes and offences have resulted. By way of reparation therefor, we have sentenced, and do hereby sentence, the said Grandier to make public apology, bareheaded, with a cord around his neck, holding a lighted torch of two pounds weight in his hand, before the west door of the church of Saint-Pierre in the Market Place and before—that of Sainte-Ursule, both of this town, and there on bended knee to ask pardon of God and the king and the law, and this done, to be taken to the public square of Sainte-Croix and there to be attached to a stake, set in the midst of a pile of wood, both of which to be prepared there for this purpose, and to be burnt alive, along with the pacts and spells which remain in the hands of the clerk and the manuscript of the book written by the said Grandier against a celibate priesthood, and his ashes, to be scattered to the four winds of heaven. And we have declared, and do hereby declare, all and every part of his property confiscate to the king, the sum of one hundred and fifty livres being first taken therefrom to be employed in the purchase of a copper plate whereon the substance of the present decree shall be engraved, the same to be exposed in a conspicuous place in the said church of Sainte-Ursule, there to remain in perpetuity; and before this sentence is carried out, we order the said Grandier to be put to the question ordinary and extraordinary, so that his accomplices may become known.

"Pronounced at Loudun against the said Grandier this 18th day of August 1634."

On the morning of the day on which this sentence was passed, M. de Laubardemont ordered the surgeon Francois Fourneau to be arrested at his own house and taken to Grandier's cell, although he was ready to go there of his own free will. In passing through the adjoining room he heard the voice of the accused saying:—

"What do you want with me, wretched executioner? Have you come to kill me? You know how cruelly you have already tortured my body. Well I am ready to die."

On entering the room, Fourneau saw that these words had been addressed to the surgeon Mannouri.

One of the officers of the 'grand privot de l'hotel', to whom M. de Laubardemont lent for the occasion the title of officer of the king's guard, ordered the new arrival to shave Grandier, and not leave a single hair on his whole body. This was a formality employed in cases of witchcraft, so that the devil should have no place to hide in; for it was the common belief that if a single hair were left, the devil could render the accused insensible to the pains of torture. From this Urbain understood that the verdict had gone against him and that he was condemned to death.

Fourneau having saluted Grandier, proceeded to carry out his orders, whereupon a judge said it was not sufficient to shave the body of the prisoner, but that his nails must also be torn out, lest the devil should hide beneath them. Grandier looked at the speaker with an expression of unutterable pity, and held out his hands to Fourneau; but Forneau put them gently aside, and said he would do nothing of the kind, even were the order given by the cardinal-duke himself, and at the same time begged Grandier's pardon for shaving him. At, these words Grandier, who had for so long met with nothing but barbarous treatment from those with whom he came in contact, turned towards the surgeon with tears in his eyes, saying—

"So you are the only one who has any pity for me."

"Ah, sir," replied F6urneau, "you don't see everybody."

Grandier was then shaved, but only two marks found on him, one as we have said on the shoulder blade, and the other on the thigh. Both marks were very sensitive, the wounds which Mannouri had made not having yet healed. This point having been certified by Fourneau, Grandier was handed, not his own clothes, but some wretched garments which had probably belonged to some other condemned man.

Then, although his sentence had been pronounced at the Carmelite convent, he was taken by the grand provost's officer, with two of his archers, accompanied by the provosts of Loudun and Chinon, to the town hall, where several ladies of quality, among them Madame de Laubardemont, led by curiosity, were sitting beside the judges, waiting to hear the sentence read. M. de Laubardemont was in the seat usually occupied by the clerk, and the clerk was standing before him. All the approaches were lined with soldiers.

Before the accused was brought in, Pere Lactance and another Franciscan who had come with him exorcised him to oblige the devils to leave him; then entering the judgment hall, they exorcised the earth, the air, "and the other elements." Not till that was done was Grandier led in.

At first he was kept at the far end of the hall, to allow time for the exorcisms to have their full effect, then he was brought forward to the bar and ordered to kneel down. Grandier obeyed, but could remove neither his hat nor his skull-cap, as his hands were bound behind his back, whereupon the clerk seized on the one and the provost's officer on the other, and flung them at de Laubardemont's feet. Seeing that the accused fixed his eyes on the commissioner as if waiting to see what he was about to do, the clerk said

"Turn your head, unhappy man, and adore the crucifix above the bench."

Grandier obeyed without a murmur and with great humility, and remained sunk in silent prayer for about ten minutes; he then resumed his former attitude.

The clerk then began to read the sentence in a trembling voice, while Grandier listened with unshaken firmness and wonderful tranquillity, although it was the most terrible sentence that could be passed, condemning the accused to be burnt alive the same day, after the infliction of ordinary and extraordinary torture. When the clerk had ended, Grandier said, with a voice unmoved from its usual calm

"Messeigneurs, I aver in the name of the Father, the Son, and the Holy Ghost, and the Blessed Virgin, my only hope, that I have never been a magician, that I have never committed sacrilege, that I know no other magic than that of the Holy Scriptures, which I have always preached, and that I have never held any other belief than that of our Holy Mother the Catholic Apostolic Church of Rome; I renounce the devil and all his works; I confess my Redeemer, and I pray to be saved through the blood of the Cross; and I beseech you, messeigneurs, to mitigate the rigour of my sentence, and not to drive my soul to despair."

The concluding words led de Laubardemont to believe that he could obtain some admission from Grandier through fear of suffering, so he ordered the court to be cleared, and, being left alone with Maitre Houmain, criminal lieutenant of Orleans, and the Franciscans, he addressed Grandier in a stern voice, saying there was only one way to obtain any mitigation of his sentence, and that was to confess the names of his accomplices and to sign the confession. Grandier replied that having committed no crime he could have no accomplices, whereupon Laubardemont ordered the prisoner to be taken to the torture chamber, which adjoined the judgment hall—an order which was instantly obeyed.

Urbain Grandier

Chapter XI

The mode of torture employed at Loudun was a variety of the boot, and one of the most painful of all. Each of the victim's legs below the knee was placed between two boards, the two pairs were then laid one above the other and bound together firmly at the ends; wedges were then driven in with a mallet between the two middle boards; four such wedges constituted ordinary and eight extraordinary torture; and this latter was seldom inflicted, except on those condemned to death, as almost no one ever survived it, the sufferer's legs being crushed to a pulp before he left the torturer's bands. In this case M. de Laubardemont on his own initiative, for it had never been done before, added two wedges to those of the extraordinary torture, so that instead of eight, ten were to be driven in.

Nor was this all: the commissioner royal and the two Franciscans undertook to inflict the torture themselves.

Laubardemont ordered Grandier to be bound in the usual manner, I and then saw his legs placed between the boards. He then dismissed the executioner and his assistants, and directed the keeper of the instruments to bring the wedges, which he complained of as being too small. Unluckily, there were no larger ones in stock, and in spite of threats the keeper persisted in saying he did not know where to procure others. M. de Laubardemont then asked how long it would take to make some, and was told two hours; finding that too long to wait, he was obliged to put up with those he had.

Thereupon the torture began. Pere Lactance having exorcised the instruments, drove in the first wedge, but could not draw a murmur from Grandier, who was reciting a prayer in a low voice; a second was driven home, and this time the victim, despite his resolution, could not avoid interrupting his devotions by two groans, at each of which Pere Lactance struck harder, crying, "Dicas! dicas!" (Confess, confess!), a word which he repeated so often and so furiously, till all was over, that he was ever after popularly called " Pere Dicas."

When the second wedge was in, de Laubardemont showed Grandier his manuscript against the celibacy of the priests, and asked if he acknowledged it to be in his own handwriting. Grandier answered in the affirmative. Asked what motive he had in writing it, he said it was an attempt to restore peace of mind to a poor girl whom he had loved, as was proved by the two lines written at the end—

*"Si ton gentil esprit prend bien cette science,
Tu mettras en repos ta bonne conscience."*

[*If thy sensitive mind imbibe this teaching,
It will give ease to thy tender conscience*]

Upon this, M. de Laubardemont demanded the girl's name; but Grandier assured him it should never pass his lips, none knowing it but himself and God. Thereupon M. de Laubardemont ordered Pere Lactance to insert the third wedge. While it was being driven in by the monk's lusty arm, each blow being accompanied by the word "'Dicas'!" Grandier exclaimed—

"My God! they are killing me, and yet I am neither a sorcerer nor sacrilegious!"

At the fourth wedge Grandier fainted, muttering—

"Oh, Pere Lactance, is this charity?"

Although his victim was unconscious, Pere Lactance continued to strike; so that, having lost consciousness through pain, pain soon brought him back to life.

De Laubardemont took advantage of this revival to take his turn at demanding a confession of his crimes; but Grandier said—

"I have committed no crimes, sir, only errors. Being a man, I have often gone astray; but I have confessed and done penance, and believe that my prayers for pardon have been heard; but if not, I trust that God will grant me pardon now, for the sake of my sufferings."

At the fifth wedge Grandier fainted once more, but they restored him to consciousness by dashing cold water in his face, whereupon he moaned, turning to M. de Laubardemont

"In pity, sir, put me to death at once! I am only a man, and I cannot answer for myself that if you continue to torture me so I shall not give way to despair."

"Then sign this, and the torture shall cease," answered the commissioner royal, offering him a paper.

"My father," said Urbain, turning towards the Franciscan, "can you assure me on your conscience that it is permissible for a man, in order to escape suffering, to confess a crime he has never committed?"

"No," replied the monk; "for if he die with a lie on his lips he dies in mortal sin."

"Go on, then," said Grandier; "for having suffered so much in my body, I desire to save my soul."

As Pere Lactance drove in the sixth wedge Grandier fainted anew.

When he had been revived, Laubardemont called upon him to confess that a certain Elisabeth Blanchard had been his mistress, as well as the girl for whom he had written the treatise against celibacy; but Grandier replied that not only had no improper relations ever existed between them, but that the day he had been confronted with her at his trial was the first time he had ever seen her.

At the seventh wedge Grandier's legs burst open, and the blood spurted into Pere Lactance's face; but he wiped it away with the sleeve of his gown.

"O Lord my God, have mercy on me! I die!" cried Grandier, and fainted for the fourth time. Pere Lactance seized the opportunity to take a short rest, and sat down.

When Grandier had once more come to himself, he began slowly to utter a prayer, so beautiful and so moving that the provost's lieutenant wrote it down; but de Laubardemont noticing this, forbade him ever to show it to anyone.

At the eighth wedge the bones gave way, and the marrow oozed out of the wounds, and it became useless to drive in any more wedges, the legs being now as flat as the boards that compressed them, and moreover Pere Lactance was quite worn out.

Grandier was unbound and laid upon the flagged floor, and while his eyes shone with fever and agony he prayed again a second prayer—a veritable martyr's prayer, overflowing with faith and enthusiasm; but as he ended his strength failed, and he again became unconscious. The provost's lieutenant forced a little wine between his lips, which brought him to; then he made an act of contrition, renounced Satan and all his works once again, and commended his soul to God.

Four men entered, his legs were freed from the boards, and the crushed parts were found to be a mere inert mass, only attached to the knees by the sinews. He was then carried to the council chamber, and laid on a little straw before the fire.

In a corner of the fireplace an Augustinian monk was seated. Urbain asked leave to confess to him, which de Laubardemont refused, holding out the paper he desired to have signed once more, at which Grandier said—

"If I would not sign to spare myself before, am I likely to give way now that only death remains?"

"True," replied Laubardemont; "but the mode of your death is in our hands: it rests with us to make it slow or quick, painless or agonising; so take this paper and sign?

Grandier pushed the paper gently away, shaking his head in sign of refusal, whereupon de Laubardemont left the room in a fury, and ordered Peres Tranquille and Claude to be admitted, they being the confessors he had chosen for Urbain. When they came near to fulfil their office, Urbain recognised in them two of his torturers, so he said that, as it was only four days since he had confessed to Pere Grillau, and he did not believe he had committed any mortal sin since then, he would not trouble them, upon which they cried out at him as a heretic and infidel, but without any effect.

At four o'clock the executioner's assistants came to fetch him; he was placed lying on a bier and carried out in that position. On the way he met the criminal lieutenant of Orleans, who once more exhorted him to confess his crimes openly; but Grandier replied—

"Alas, sir, I have avowed them all; I have kept nothing back."

"Do you desire me to have masses said for you?" continued the lieutenant.

"I not only desire it, but I beg for it as a great favour," said Urbain.

A lighted torch was then placed in his hand: as the procession started he pressed the torch to his lips; he looked on all whom he met with modest confidence, and begged those whom he knew to intercede with God for him. On the threshold of the door his sentence was read to him, and he was then placed in a small cart and driven to the church of St. Pierre in the market-place. There he was awaited by M. de Laubardemont, who ordered him to alight. As he could not stand on his mangled limbs, he was pushed out, and fell first on his knees and then on his face. In this position he remained patiently waiting to be lifted. He was carried to the top of the steps and laid down, while his sentence was read to him once more, and just as it was finished, his confessor, who had not been allowed to see him for four days, forced a way through the crowd and threw himself into Grandier's arms. At first tears choked Pere Grillau's voice, but at last he said, "Remember, sir, that our Saviour Jesus Christ ascended to His Father through the agony of the Cross: you are a wise man, do not give way now and lose everything. I bring you your mother's blessing; she and I never cease to pray that God may have mercy on you and receive you into Paradise."

These words seemed to inspire Grandier with new strength; he lifted his head, which pain had bowed, and raising his eyes to heaven, murmured a short prayer. Then turning towards the worthy, friar, he said—

"Be a son to my mother; pray to God for me constantly; ask all our good friars to pray for my soul; my one consolation is that I die innocent. I trust that God in His mercy may receive me into Paradise."

"Is there nothing else I can do for you?" asked Pére Grillau.

"Alas, my father!" replied Grandier, "I am condemned to die a most cruel death; ask the executioner if there is no way of shortening what I must undergo."

"I go at once," said the friar; and giving him absolution in 'articulo mortis', he went down the steps, and while Grandier was making his confession aloud the good monk drew the executioner aside and asked if there were no possibility of alleviating the death-agony by means of a shirt dipped in brimstone. The executioner answered that as the sentence expressly stated that Grandier was to be burnt alive, he could not employ an expedient so sure to be discovered as that; but that if the friar would give him thirty crowns he would undertake to strangle Grandier while he was kindling the pile. Pere Grillau gave him the money, and the executioner provided himself with a rope. The Franciscan then placed himself where he could speak to his penitent as he passed, and as he embraced him for the last time, whispered to him what he had arranged with the executioner, whereupon Grandier turned towards the latter and said in a tone of deep gratitude—

"Thanks, my brother."

At that moment, the archers having driven away Pere Grillau, by order of M. de Laubardemont, by beating him with their halberts, the procession resumed its march, to go through the same ceremony at the Ursuline church, and from there to proceed to the square of Sainte- Croix. On the way Urbain met and recognised Moussant, who was accompanied by his wife, and turning towards him, said—

"I die your debtor, and if I have ever said a word that could offend you I ask you to forgive me."

When the place of execution was reached, the provost's lieutenant approached Grandier and asked his forgiveness.

"You have not offended me," was the reply; "you have only done what your duty obliged you to do."

The executioner then came forward and removed the back board of the cart, and ordered his assistants to carry Grandier to where the pile was prepared. As he was unable to stand, he was attached to the stake by an iron hoop passed round his body. At that moment a flock of pigeons seemed to fall from the sky, and, fearless of the crowd, which was so great that the archers could not succeed even by blows of their weapons in clearing a way for the magistrates, began to fly around Grandier, while one, as white as the driven snow, alighted on the summit of the stake, just above his head. Those who believed in possession exclaimed that they were only a band of devils come to seek their master, but there were many who muttered that devils were not wont to assume such a form, and who persisted in believing that the doves had come in default of men to bear witness to Grandier's innocence.

In trying next day to combat this impression, a monk asserted that he had seen a huge fly buzzing round Grandier's head, and as

Beelzebub meant in Hebrew, as he said, the god of flies, it was quite evident that it was that demon himself who, taking upon him the form of one of his subjects, had come to carry off the magician's soul.

When everything was prepared, the executioner passed the rope by which he meant to strangle him round Grandier's neck; then the priests exorcised the earth, air, and wood, and again demanded of their victim if he would not publicly confess his crimes. Urbain replied that he had nothing to say, but that he hoped through the martyr's death he was about to die to be that day with Christ in Paradise.

The clerk then read his sentence to him for the fourth time, and asked if he persisted in what he said under torture.

"Most certainly I do," said Urbain; "for it was the exact truth."

Upon this, the clerk withdrew, first informing Grandier that if he had anything to say to the people he was at liberty to speak.

But this was just what the exorcists did not want: they knew Grandier's eloquence and courage, and a firm, unshaken denial at the moment of death would be most prejudicial to their interests. As soon, therefore, as Grandier opened his lips to speak, they dashed such a quantity of holy water in his face that it took away his breath. It was but for a moment, however, and he recovered himself, and again endeavoured to speak, a monk stooped down and stifled the words by kissing him on the lips. Grandier, guessing his intention, said loud enough for those next the pile to hear, "That was the kiss of Judas!"

At these words the monks become so enraged that one of them struck Grandier three times in the face with a crucifix, while he appeared to be giving it him to kiss; but by the blood that flowed from his nose and lips at the third blow those standing near perceived the truth: all Grandier could do was to call out that he asked for a Salve Regina and an Ave Maria, which many began at once to repeat, whilst he with clasped hands and eyes raised to heaven commended himself to God and the Virgin. The exorcists then made one more effort to get him to confess publicly, but he exclaimed—

"My fathers, I have said all I had to say; I hope in God and in His mercy."

At this refusal the anger of the exorcists surpassed all bounds, and Pere Lactance, taking a twist of straw, dipped it in a bucket of pitch which was standing beside the pile, and lighting it at a torch, thrust it into his face, crying—

"Miserable wretch! will nothing force you to confess your crimes and renounce the devil?"

"I do not belong to the devil," said Grandier, pushing away the straw with his hands; "I have renounced the devil, I now renounce him and all his works again, and I pray that God may have mercy on me."

At this, without waiting for the signal from the provost's lieutenant, Pere Lactance poured the bucket of pitch on one corner of the pile of wood and set fire to it, upon which Grandier called the executioner to his aid, who, hastening up, tried in vain to strangle him, while the flames spread apace.

"Ah! my brother," said the sufferer, "is this the way you keep your promise?"

"It's not my fault," answered the executioner; "the monks have knotted the cord, so that the noose cannot slip."

"Oh, Father Lactance! Father Lactance! have you no charity?" cried Grandier.

The executioner by this time was forced by the increasing heat to jump down from the pile, being indeed almost overcome; and seeing this, Grandier stretched forth a hand into the flames, and said—

"Pere Lactance, God in heaven will judge between thee and me; I summon thee to appear before Him in thirty days."

Grandier was then seen to make attempts to strangle himself, but either because it was impossible, or because he felt it would be wrong to end his life by his own hands, he desisted, and clasping his hands, prayed aloud—

"Deus meus, ad te vigilo, miserere me."

A Capuchin fearing that he would have time to say more, approached the pile from the side which had not yet caught fire, and dashed the remainder of the holy water in his face. This caused such smoke that Grandier was hidden for a moment from the eyes of the spectators; when it cleared away, it was seen that his clothes were now alight; his voice could still be heard from the midst of the flames raised in prayer; then three times, each time in a weaker voice, he pronounced the name of Jesus, and giving one cry, his head fell forward on his breast.

At that moment the pigeons which had till then never ceased to circle round the stake, flew away, and were lost in the clouds.

Urbain Grandier had given up the ghost.

Chapter XII

This time it was not the man who was executed who was guilty, but the executioners; consequently we feel sure that our readers will be anxious to learn something of their fate.

Pere Lactance died in the most terrible agony on September 18th, 1634, exactly a month from the date of Grandier's death. His brother-monks considered that this was due to the vengeance of Satan; but others were not wanting who said, remembering the summons uttered by Grandier, that it was rather due to the justice of God. Several attendant circumstances seemed to favour the latter opinion. The author of the History of the Devils of Loudzin gives an account of one of these circumstances, for the authenticity of which he vouches, and from which we extract the following:

"Some days after the execution of Grandier, Pere Lactance fell ill of the disease of which he died. Feeling that it was of supernatural origin, he determined to take a pilgrimage to Notre Dame des Andilliers de Saumur, where many miracles were wrought, and which was held in high estimation in the neighbourhood. A place in the carriage of the Sieur de Canaye was offered him for the journey; for this gentleman, accompanied by a large party on pleasure bent, was just then setting out for his estate of Grand Fonds, which lay in the same direction. The reason for the offer was that Canaye and his friends, having heard that the last words of Grandier had affected Pere Lactance's mind, expected to find a great deal of amusement in exciting the terrors of their travelling-companion. And in truth, for a day or two, the boon companions sharpened their wits at the expense of the worthy monk, when all at once, on a good road and without apparent cause, the carriage overturned. Though no one was hurt, the accident appeared so strange to the pleasure-seekers that it put an end to the jokes of even the boldest among them. Pere Lactance himself appeared melancholy and preoccupied, and that evening at supper refused to eat, repeating over and over again—

"'It was wrong of me to deny Grandier the confessor he asked for; God is punishing me, God is punishing me!'

"On the following morning the journey was resumed, but the evident distress of mind under which Pere Lactance laboured had so damped the spirits of the party that all their gaiety had disappeared. Suddenly, just outside Fenet, where the road was in excellent condition and no obstacle to their progress apparent, the carriage upset for the second time. Although again no one was hurt, the travellers felt that there was among them someone against whom God's anger was turned, and their suspicions pointing to Pere Lactance, they went on their way, leaving him behind, and feeling very uncomfortable at the thought that they had spent two or three days in his society.

Pere Lactance at last reached Notre-Dame des Andilliers; but however numerous were the miracles there performed, the remission of the doom pronounced by the martyr on Pere Lactance was not added to their number; and at a quarter-past six on September 18th, exactly a month to the very minute after Grandier's death, Pere Lactance expired in excruciating agony."

Pere Tranquille's turn came four years later. The malady which attacked him was so extraordinary that the physicians were quite at a loss, and forced to declare their ignorance of any remedy. His shrieks and blasphemies were so distinctly heard in the streets, that his brother Franciscans, fearing the effect they would have on his after-reputation, especially in the minds of those who had seen Grandier die with words of prayer on his lips, spread abroad the report that the devils whom he had expelled from the bodies of the nuns had entered into the body of the exorcist. He died shrieking—

"My God! how I suffer! Not all the devils and all the damned together endure what I endure!" His panegyrist, in whose book we find all the horrible details of his death employed to much purpose to illustrate the advantages of belonging to the true faith, remarks—

Urbain Grandier

"Truly big generous heart must have been a hot hell for those fiends who entered his body to torment it."

The following epitaph which was placed over his grave was interpreted, according to the prepossessions of those who read it, either as a testimony to his sanctity or as a proof of his punishment:—

"Here lies Pere Tranquille, of Saint-Remi; a humble Capuchin preacher. The demons no longer able to endure his fearlessly exercised power as an exorcist, and encouraged by sorcerers, tortured him to death, on May 31st, 1638."

But a death about which there could be no doubt as to the cause was that of the surgeon Mannouri, the same who had, as the reader may recollect, been the first to torture Grandier. One evening about ten o'clock he was returning from a visit to a patient who lived on the outskirts of the town, accompanied by a colleague and preceded by his surgery attendant carrying a lantern. When they reached the centre of the town in the rue Grand-Pave, which passes between the walls of the castle grounds and the gardens of the Franciscan monastery, Mannouri suddenly stopped, and, staring fixedly at some object which was invisible to his companions, exclaimed with a start—

"Oh! there is Grandier!"

"Where? where?" cried the others.

He pointed in the direction towards which his eyes were turned, and beginning to tremble violently, asked—

"What do you want with me, Grandier? What do you want?"

A moment later he added

"Yes-yes, I am coming."

Urbain Grandier

Immediately it seemed as if the vision vanished from before his eyes, but the effect remained. His brother-surgeon and the servant brought him home, but neither candles nor the light of day could allay his fears; his disordered brain showed him Grandier ever standing at the foot of his bed. A whole week he continued, as was known all over the town, in this condition of abject terror; then the spectre seemed to move from its place and gradually to draw nearer, for he kept on repeating, "He is coming! he is coming!" and at length, towards evening, at about the same hour at which Grandier expired, Surgeon Mannouri drew his last breath.

We have still to tell of M. de Laubardemont. All we know is thus related in the letters of M. de Patin:—

> "On the 9th inst., at nine o'clock in the evening, a carriage was attacked by robbers; on hearing the noise the townspeople ran to the spot, drawn thither as much by curiosity as by humanity. A few shots were exchanged and the robbers put to flight, with the exception of one man belonging to their band who was taken prisoner, and another who lay wounded on the paving-stones. This latter died next day without having spoken, and left no clue behind as to who he was. His identity was, however, at length made clear. He was the son of a high dignitary named de Laubardemont, who in 1634, as royal commissioner, condemned Urbain Grandier, a poor, priest of Loudun, to be burnt alive, under the pretence that he had caused several nuns of Loudun to be possessed by devils. These nuns he had so tutored as to their behaviour that many people foolishly believed them to be demoniacs. May we not regard the fate of his son as a chastisement inflicted by Heaven on this unjust judge—an expiation exacted for the pitilessly cruel death inflicted on his victim, whose blood still cries unto the Lord from the ground?"

Naturally the persecution of Urbain Grandier attracted the attention not only of journalists but of poets. Among the many poems which were inspired by it, the following is one of the best. Urbain speaks:—

Urbain Grandier

"From hell came the tidings that by horrible sanctions
I had made a pact with the devil to have power over women:
Though not one could be found to accuse me.
In the trial which delivered me to torture and the stake,
The demon who accused me invented and suggested the crime,

And his testimony was the only proof against me.

The English in their rage burnt the Maid alive;
Like her, I too fell a victim to revenge;
We were both accused falsely of the same crime;
In Paris she is adored, in London abhorred;
In Loudun some hold me guilty of witchcraft,
Some believe me innocent; some halt between two minds.

Like Hercules, I loved passionately;
Like him, I was consumed by fire;
But he by death became a god.
The injustice of my death was so well concealed
That no one can judge whether the flames saved or destroyed me;
Whether they blackened me for hell, or purified me for heaven.

In vain did I suffer torments with unshaken resolution;
They said that I felt no pain, being a sorcerer died unrepentant;
That the prayers I uttered were impious words;
That in kissing the image on the cross I spat in its face;
That casting my eyes to heaven I mocked the saints;
That when I seemed to call on God, I invoked the devil

Others, more charitable, say, in spite of their hatred of my crime,
That my death may be admired although my life was not blameless;
That my resignation showed that I died in hope and faith;
That to forgive, to suffer without complaint or murmur,
Is perfect love; and that the soul is purified
From the sins of life by a death like mine."

End

Lightning Source UK Ltd.
Milton Keynes UK
UKHW011259081221
395308UK00001B/64